Little House in the Rain Forest

An Adventure Story...

by Kathy Slamp, M.Ed.

Dedication

To...
My two grandsons,
Preston and Braeden.

May their childhoods be filled
with innocence and joy.

Other Books by Kathy Slamp

Little House in the Arctic

Remdezvous with Majesty

A Picnic at the Glacier

Majesty Alaska DVD

Walking through Life without Stumbling

Reflection Profiles

The Word in Real Time

You Might Be a Pastor's Wife If...

Mastering Women's Ministries

Contents

Chapter 1: Leaving our Little House 1

Chapter 2: The Trip "Outside" 11

Chapter 3: The Summer of 1952 23

Chapter 4: Traveling Eastward 35

Chapter 5: A Side Trip to New York 45

Chapter 6: More Traveling 53

Chapter 7: A Year in Ohio 63

Chapter 8: The Summer of 1953 75

Chapter 9: Back to Alaska 89

Chapter 10: The Boarding House 99

Chapter 11: Historic Juneau 111

Chapter 12: A House of our Own 125

Chapter 13: Shipwrecks & Plane Crashes 137

Chapter 14: Sunshine Holidays 147

Chapter 15: Tragedy Close to Home 161

Chapter 16: Missing Pieces 171

Chapter 17: Back to the States 181

Appendix and Acknowledgements 191

To the Reader

Little House in the Rain Forest is a continuation of the story of my Alaskan childhood. It is a sequel to my first Alaska book, *Little House in the Arctic.* Our family moved to Alaska from Texas immediately after World War II, but after five delightful years in Fairbanks, we returned to the states. Alaska was in our blood, though, and we didn't stay away long. After one adventure-filled year of traveling and resettling in the Eastern part of the United States, we packed up and moved back to Alaska—this time to Juneau in the temperate rain forest of the Southeast.

Little House in the Rain Forest is a true story of adventure written for children of all ages. Life in Juneau was drastically different than life in Fairbanks. In Juneau we faced challenges of monstrous proportions that could have destroyed a less determined family unit. Although our years in Juneau were enchanting ones as we romped and played around glaciers and climbed world-class mountains, they presented many challenges as well. It was in Juneau that I first faced issues of life and death, along with the day-to-day struggles of approaching adolescence and adulthood. It was there that I began to "grow up."

This book is written as a direct response from hundreds of readers requesting a sequel to *Little House in the Arctic.* I don't think you will be disappointed.

Chapter 1
Leaving Our Little House

In the spring of 1952, it hardly seemed possible that out lives were radically changing again, but they were. It had been five full years since the fall of 1947 when my parents packed up the five of us and moved our family half way around the world from the Rio Grande Valley in South Texas to the frigid northland—specifically Fairbanks, Alaska. What a move that was! We moved to Fairbanks in October 1947, and from that day until the spring of 1952, our lives were completely rearranged.

Our move to Alaska was good; it was exciting; and it quickly became normal for our family. After five years in the far north, all of us had acclimated well to the harsh, yet stimulating, climate of Alaska's interior. The extreme weather challenges, coupled with the remoteness of the region were offset by Alaskans' warmth and sense of adventure. Our family of five had come to know, love, and be a part of the whole ambience of Alaska. My father was a Protestant minister, and we moved to Alaska when he was appointed by his denomination to relocate to this far flung outpost as a missionary.

He wasn't obligated to accept the position, but my parents' sense of adventure inspired them to rise to the challenge. They were young; they were adventuresome; and we all fell in love with Alaska.

When we left Texas in 1947 my baby brother, Sammy, was only two weeks old; he was exactly three weeks old when we landed in Fairbanks. Alaska was absolutely all little Sammy knew. Moving to Alaska precipitated many changes for my older brother, Jason, and me. Jason transferred to Alaska in the middle of his third grade year, and the second year we were in Fairbanks, I began school. In the spring of 1952, when we moved back "outside," I was set to begin the fourth grade, and Jason was going into the seventh. The single school in Fairbanks that housed all grades from kindergarten through high school had been our only academic home; we loved it and our teachers.

In those days, Alaska's educational system was one of the best in the United States—even though Alaska was not a state, but a territory. Jason and I were both good students, and everyone in the school knew who we were. We participated in all the music programs and the May pole dances. We were both survivors of the 1949 polio epidemic that closed our school for three weeks and took the lives of several of our classmates as well as leaving some in iron lungs. Our school house that today serves as the Fairbanks City Hall was a big and exciting element of our young lives.

The entire five years that our family lived in Fairbanks, we lived in the little one bedroom house next door to Dad's mission church on the corner of Tenth and Noble streets. We three kids shared the basement with the laundry facilities, where we adapted to sleeping with racks of drying clothes on folding racks that Mother strewed around our basement world. There was a huge difference between Alaska and Texas—bigger by far than size.

Our eating habits changed drastically in 1947 when we moved from Texas to Alaska. In Texas the milkman came every morning with fresh milk and butter, but in Alaska we learned to drink and cook with diluted canned milk. In the Rio Grande Valley, we were accustomed to fresh fruit and vegetables anytime we wanted them. San Antonio was then, and still is today, a hub of Mexican/American blended cultures; therefore, in Texas we could get good Tex/Mex. Fortunately for us, Mother learned to cook Mexican food well; thus, we were able to have it from time to time in Fairbanks—that is when Mother could get someone to ship or bring her a vacuum packed can of tortillas.

In Alaska our diet changed from a fresh fruit and vegetable diet to one of root vegetables such as potatoes, carrots, rutabagas and the like. In the short, but beautiful, Alaskan summers Mother quickly learned that there was a veritable plethora of available berries. After our first Alaskan winter, our family joined hundreds of others who headed for the brush, fighting mosquitoes the size of Volkswagen Beetles in order to pick world class blueberries, cranberries, raspberries, and rosehips. Every now and then, Mother even used her southern cooking knowledge that she learned as a girl in Oklahoma and cooked us a "mess" of Alaskan greens. She couldn't get collards, but she learned to cook dandelion greens just as well, and they were pretty good—most of the time, that is.

In South Texas my older brother Jason and I never even owned a sweater. We romped and played in the humid South Texas sunshine, visited the Breckenridge Park and Zoo, and spent summer evenings chasing fire flies. None of this was possible in Alaska, but we didn't feel deprived. Living in Alaska was just different; that's all. In Alaska we had to bundle up in layers and layers of clothing just to walk the two short blocks to school. Every inch of us (including our mouth and nose) had to be covered to protect us from the miserable and defying cold.

In contrast to the wet, humid air of Southeast Alaska, the air in Alaska's interior is dry, causing temperatures to be deceptive. One day, for example, I walked home two blocks from the school's ice skating rink—*on* my skates. In the unheated ice skating house, I tried to unlace them, but it was so cold that I thought I could wobble the two blocks home on my skates. They weren't laced up well, though, and the back of my ankles were exposed. In that short two block walk, I developed a slight frost bite on both of my heals. That small, but potentially devastating, incident taught me a huge personal lesson about Alaska's brutal cold.

Despite the bleak, miserably cold and incessant winter hours of darkness, life in our *Little House in the Arctic* was neither bleak nor dark. Mother and Dad kept our little house and our little lives lively. The size of the house didn't faze my mother. Often, she cooked meals on the "modern" oil stove for dozens of service personnel, government workers, people from Dad's little mission church, or visitors from the lower forty-eight—*outsiders*, we called them.

We spent warm evenings indoors on cold nights playing games, popping gallons of popcorn, or reading. My father's love of books and literature inspired both Jason and me to read. Saturdays we made frequent trips to the library and brought home armloads of books to read during the week. On many winter nights, Dad read to all of us from the classics, introducing us to Charles Dickens, Aesop's fables, and other familiar children's books such as *Heidi, Bob—Son of Battle,* and *The Five Little Peppers.*

Mom and Dad weren't afraid to venture out in the harsh winters, either. Our family attended the famous Fairbanks Winter

Carnival that was held each year on the Chena River. That's right, *on* the river. At the carnival, we stood shoulder to shoulder with military personnel from every state in the union and indigenous Alaskan natives whose ancestors had somewhere in the distant past crossed the land bridge between Siberia and Alaska. These Native Americans had lived in this environment for generations, and we quickly grew accustomed to seeing them in their native garbs. Our first winter, however, everyone in our family was called a *chichaca*—a Native American word that means "newcomer."

The Winter Carnival was truly a multi-cultural experience; no one in those days even gave a second thought to the fact that we were participating in something so "politically correct." With its Eskimo Olympics, the carnival was merely an opportunity for all of us to break the winter boredom and sense of isolation that comes from day after day of continual darkness. It was at these carnivals that Jason and I were introduced to dogsled racing, the blanket toss, and numerous other Native American traditions. Somewhere along the line, someone taught us both how to manipulate the "Eskimo yo-yo." Operating this unique yo-yo is like riding a bike; it seems hard at first, but once you master the skill, you never forget it. The third year we were in Fairbanks, Mother bought some used fur coats and made us all authentic Alaskan parkas. We really fit into the atmosphere of Alaska after that.

When Jason and Sammy and I were young, my father was a restless sort. In those days it wasn't customary for pastors or missionaries to stay in one place for several years like it is today. After nearly five years in Fairbanks, Dad thought we should move back to the lower forty-eight. No one in his mission congregation, or the greater Fairbanks metropolitan area for that matter, wanted Dad to move. He was both loved by his parishioners and respected by the city at large. During those five years, Dad was extremely active in Kiwanis Club and the local ministerial association. He became well known throughout the community. Dad's little "flock" (which wasn't nearly so small after five years of his hard work) wrote a petition that was signed by every single member and friend of the church begging him to reconsider and stay in Fairbanks longer.

But, in the spring of 1952, Dad would not be dissuaded, and plans were made for a move. Dad was sincere in his desire to move—with one exception: He had no place to go. It was an odd position to be in; he had a job that people were begging him to keep, but he felt that he must resign to take an unknown job that he was certain God would provide.

In anticipation of that move, our last year in Fairbanks was a great deal different than the first four. Mother went to work. That was a novel thing for us kids because all of our lives up to that point, she was a "stay at home mom." The little mission in Fairbanks provided our family the little house and all its furnishings. Consequently, when we moved to Alaska in 1947, we left everything but the basic essentials behind. Mother and Dad knew that a return to the lower forty-eight meant we would most likely have a parsonage provided, but there would be no furniture. So, Mother went to work to save money for purchasing furniture when we moved to the yet undisclosed location.

Mother was a good bookkeeper, and soon she got an excellent job with Pan American World Airways—the same airline that flew us to Alaska in 1947. In the early 50's things were still a bit makeshift in Alaska, and although Mother's job was a good one, it wasn't in a nice building. Mother's office was a small cubicle that had been built sometime during the war at the back of an old hangar. Each day that she went to work she had to pass through the massive building with its collection of discarded and wrecked airplanes just to get to her office.

Because of Alaska's remoteness and the expense of living so far from the heart of production, everything in Alaska carried an exorbitant price tag—especially fresh milk, and fresh fruits and vegetables. For five years our family had grown accustomed to eating root vegetables during the winter and augmenting our diet in the summer with an array of fresh berries. We had been drinking and cooking with canned milk for so long that none of us could even remember the taste of fresh milk. Mother's job at Pan American, though, offered her one amazing "perk."

Pan Am was a worldwide airline that flew back and forth from Seattle every single day. On those trips they always delivered an eye-popping selection of fresh fruits, vegetables, and milk to Fairbanks grocery stores. Because of their high cost, these items were taboo to us. Pan Am, though, had a commissary that was available to all its workers at reasonable to nearly free costs. So, the last year we spent in Fairbanks, our family ate like most of the families in the lower forty-eight. We had fresh lettuce salads, oranges and bananas in abundance—*and* fresh milk. What a treat. For the first month that Mother worked for Pan Am, these fresh foods nearly spoiled in our "ice box" because we were so afraid to eat them. Shortly, though, we got the hang of it, and what a special year that was. It seemed to Jason and me that we had joined the ranks of the elite once we were able to eat so well.

Mother and Dad continued steadfast in their determination to return to the lower forty-eight, despite the fact that Dad had a great job in Fairbanks and none anywhere else. He spoke with his denominational supervisor who appointed him to Fairbanks in 1947 and explained his feelings of restlessness. He felt, he said, that his job in Fairbanks was finished. Dad's supervisor seemed to understand, and although he knew Dad and Mother were loved and respected in Fairbanks, he honored Dad's feelings as well and promised to find him a good position—he would just have to wait.

The people in Dad's little mission church, though, didn't think he was finished—not at all. To a person they loved and respected both Dad and Mother. When he arrived in 1947, the church was small and still dependent on the mother denomination for financial support. They owned a fine piece of property on the corner of Tenth and Noble streets that housed the little church, our *Little House in the Arctic*, a rustic log cabin, and a tiny rental. The church had few attendees when Dad arrived in 1947. Lack of attendance never deterred my Dad; he and Mother went to work immediately upon landing in Alaska, and the results of their labors were phenomenal. They didn't do all the work, of course, but my father's sense of enthusiasm and creativity coupled with my mother's sense of adventure were contagious. In short order, the little church was financially independent, and after five years, it had doubled more than once.

At last, Dad's supervisor called with his new assignment. He was being sent to a large church in Southern Ohio right on the Ohio River. At that time, my parents had never been east of Kansas City, and, of course, none of the three of us kids had either. Dad trusted his supervisor implicitly, and he and Mother approached this new assignment with their customary excitement and adventure. Their families didn't get it, though. They thought that moving to Ohio from Alaska in 1952 was more absurd than our moving to Alaska from Texas in 1947. Mom and Dad weren't fazed by their families' protestations.

Moving back to the lower forty-eight was what they felt they should do, and off we went.

Ohio would prove to be just as different for us as Alaska had been. Dad's new church was completely different also, but all that lay ahead. For the time being, our family focused on leaving Alaska and putting that chapter of our lives behind us forever.

Chapter 2
The Trip "Outside"

In addition to setting aside money to purchase furniture for our new home in a city that wasn't even decided yet, Mother and Dad had other plans for her Pan Am earnings. In the spring of 1952, they thought that since we were leaving Alaska for good, it would be great to take our family outside on a steamship. This was most definitely impossible on Dad's meager salary, but it was a real possibility now that Mother had such a good job. During the winter of 1951 and 1952, Mother and Dad saved nearly every cent Mother earned for a "trip of a lifetime" as well as for new furniture—furniture of our very own.

In the twenty-first century, Alaska cruise passengers spend their week on large cruise ships with several thousand other passengers. Modern ships include all the amenities of a first class resort: beauty parlors, fully furnished health and fitness spas, casinos, libraries, multiple dining facilities, child care centers, teen activities, photography studios, wedding chapels, dance floors, shore excursion desks, on-board boutiques, swimming pools, and miniature golf courses. In addition to all this, there are well-appointed theaters with state-of-the art equipment where top name entertainers, ship board dancers and singers, as well as Alaska naturalists, perform daily. Today's cruise lines offer bridge classes, pottery classes, digital camera and computer seminars, and beautifully decorated rooms for private parties. Very little of this was available in 1952, but these amenities actually have no bearing on the beauty of an Alaskan cruise.

Today, there are numerous cruise line choices and diverse cruise route options. It was different in 1952. Then, there were several smaller lines, with only two main cruise line choices: The Alaska Steamship Company and the Canadian/Pacific Railroad & Steamship Company. Both of these companies had been sailing back and forth to Alaska from either Seattle or Vancouver for well over fifty years, and each of them had a colorful and historic past. Each of these lines contributed significantly to Alaska's early development, and each played a major part during the Klondike gold rush of the late 1800s. Each was used extensively by early naturalists (such as John Muir), as well as presidents and other dignitaries.

In 1894, the Alaska Steamship Company began regular service between Seattle and Alaska. Before this, the Alaska Commercial Company provided occasional steamship service to its northern trading posts. There were NO lighthouses in all of Southeast Alaska until two were built in 1902. Navigation was treacherous, and the fallout form eddies, unseen sandbars, scholes, and bad weather were both numerous and notorious. If the waterways of the Inside Passage could only talk, what stories they could tell, and what sunken treasures they could reveal.

In 1908 the Alaskan Syndicate was formed with funds from two extremely wealthy families—J.P. Morgan and the Guggenheims.

This syndicate purchased the Alaska Steamship Company, and for nearly seventy years, their "star fleet" of passenger/cargo steamships plied the waters of Southeast and South Central Alaska. Before World War II, they had forty-two vessels, but the war changed that forever. By the late forties, continued improvements on the Alaskan Railroad, emerging air traffic, and upgraded barges reduced Alaska Steamship Company's ships to only seven vessels. Cargo transport continued until 1974, but the passenger business survived only until 1954. *The Baranof*—our 1952 ship—was one of those last seven vessels.

The Baranof, like many other Alaska Steamship vessels, was conscripted for use during World War II. The U.S. government chartered these vessels and delivered battalions and regiments such as "D" Company to remote places like Cordova and Valdez. From there, these troops were deployed even further south along the Aleutian Islands where a violent battle was raging with Japan. Few people even remember it now, but after the Japanese bombed Dutch Harbor, "The Forgotten War" as it was called, roared up and down Alaska's Aleutian archipelago.

Alaska's Aleutian Islands were the only American soil occupied by the enemy during World War II, and hundreds of Americans and Japanese alike succumbed to the elements in these remote and weather-battered islands—either to the battle or the weather. When it was all said and done, the weather was the winner in this distant war. The Japanese—realizing the futility of this torturous outpost at the end of the world—fled back to Japan under cover of fog. In truth, the Japanese never realized Alaska's strategic importance. They were merely using their invasion of Alaskan soil as a diversionary tactic to deflect American ships, personnel, and supplies from the war in the South Pacific. If they had fully understood Alaska's potential, and if they could have conquered the weather, the results of World War II might have been drastically different.

The steamers that were still in operation in 1952 weren't merely for the pleasure of indulging passengers. Not at all! That type of all-consuming touring and passenger gratification didn't reach Alaska until the end of the Twentieth Century. It wasn't economically feasible or reasonable to sail a ship two thousand miles or more without carrying cargo. Consequently, these little ships carried both cargo and passengers. In actuality, these steamers were glorified cargo ships with accommodations for a few passengers. They were sturdy, dependable, and luxurious for their day.

Mother and Dad wanted to provide our family with an experience of a life time; one that we would never forget—a trip from Seward to Seattle via the Alaskan Steamship Lines. Mother's salary at Pan Am provided the necessary funds. So it was that in the spring of 1952, we sailed from Seward to Seattle on the Alaska Steamship, *the Baranof.* Our week on the *Baranof* was truly memorable in every way, but even before we boarded the boat, Mom and Dad treated us to yet another life time thrill. Rather than drive from Fairbanks to Seward (a distance of over six hundred miles), they purchased tickets on the Alaska Railroad from Fairbanks to Anchorage and then on to Seward.

I had been on the train once before in the summer of 1950 when Mother took me to Anchorage for an unforgettable hospital stay after I punctured my eardrum (see *Little House in the Arctic*, Chapter 7). Mother and Dad went by train to Mount McKinley Park in the winter of 1949 after Mother lost a baby, but the spring of 1952 was the first and last time all five of us took a train trip together. The Alaska Railroad between Seward and Fairbanks is one of the world's

Fairbanks departure – May 1952

most magnificent trips, and the beauty of that trip has not changed a whit in over fifty year.

Because the weather was clear when we departed, Mt. McKinley was the first sight we viewed as we left Fairbanks. Once you near Nenana, the mountain looks as though you could reach out and touch it even though it is still nearly a hundred miles away. At 20,050 feet high, Mt. McKinley is the tallest mountain on the North American continent, and it is so gigantic that it effectively creates its own weather. Sadly, the mountain is fogged in so often that visitors who come from thousands of miles to see it often don't even catch a glimpse of this glorious sight. Hundreds of people have attempted to scale its heights; and stories and legends of these expeditions are both captivating and heartbreaking. Viewing the mountain from the train, however, is painless and spectacular. It wasn't any less beautiful in 1952 than it is today. Pictures never do Mt. McKinley justice. You must see it "up close and personal" to truly appreciate its magnificence.

After the trained passed Mt. McKinley, we crossed Hurricane Gulch, steep mountain passes, and had whistle stops in small American Native villages and hamlets. Eventually, we chugged though Palmer—the sight of the depression era homestead settlement experiment. The Matanuska Valley is a lush area where farms are plentiful to this day, but in the 1930s, most of the original settlers left Alaska after their first miserable winter.

Anchorage was our major stop, and in 1952 it was already Alaska's largest city. When we arrived in Alaska in 1947, Dad's little mission in Fairbanks was the only one that his denomination had in Alaska except for an outpost in Nome. Five years later, things were different. His denomination now had churches in Anchorage and Seward—both of which my father was instrumental in helping organize. The pastors and their families of these churches were dear friends of ours. It seemed inconceivable that we would leave Alaska without telling our precious Alaskan friends and co-workers "good bye." Both the pastor in Anchorage and the pastor in Seward had daughters my age, and I definitely wanted to see my two friends before I left Alaska. Many years later, one of these girls and I lived in the same Midwestern town, but in 1952, I thought I would never see either of them again.

During our time in Alaska, no one we knew ever stayed in a hotel. Staying in a hotel was unthinkable for two reasons: first, the cost was prohibitive, but an even bigger factor was Alaska's famous hospitality. Regardless of the size of their house or means, Alaskans always took their friends into their homes when they came to visit from another town. Mother took in friends (and strangers as well) time and again during our years in Fairbanks, and now it was our turn to stay with friends. Friends in Alaska—especially long ago—grew closer than family. This strange closeness and family feeling was nurtured by Alaska's remoteness and its bleak living conditions.

Our family, for instance, was over 3,000 miles from home— either Oklahoma or Oregon. Nearly everyone we knew in Alaska was in the same situation. Whatever the reason, saying "good bye" in Alaska was difficult. In the spring of 1952, our family spent a couple days with our Anchorage friends talking about our times together, enjoying each other's company, and dreading that last farewell. All too quickly the day arrived, and the five of us shared tearful "good-byes" and boarded the train once again for the short half-day trip to Seward.

The train route to Seward from Anchorage follows the Turnagain Arm; it's about an hour and a half drive these days by car. Along this route is Portage Glacier, the most visited site in all of Alaska. Near the glacier, a road veers southeast toward the little city of Whittier. You must pass through one of the world's most unique tunnels in order to reach this little hamlet, Alaska's World War II military fuel depot. At one time Whittier gave Seward a run for business in South Central Alaska, but its isolation kept it from ever becoming a thriving town. After the military mothballed and deactivated Whittier in 1960, and following the 1964 earthquake that virtually destroyed the entire area, it was nearly void of all life. Nothing significant occurred in Whittier until the late 1980s when the cruise ships "discovered" it as a gateway to College Fjord.

Whittier's history, though, and its strategic location were critical during World War II and the Cold War. At one time, everyone and everything in Whittier all lived and happened in the same building—the Buckner Building. Until the early 2000s, the only ways to reach Whittier were by seaplane, ship, or via the one way rail tunnel. Today, cars can drive to Whittier via the tunnel, but it's still only a one way tunnel. You must wait at either end for a green light before you pass through this 2.6 mile tunnel dug through solid rock sixty years ago during World War II.

In the fifties, Seward was South Central Alaska's main port of entry, and it is still used today for Pacific sea traffic. Located on beautiful Resurrection Bay, Seward is a perfect year round port. Seward may get snowed in—and it does—but Resurrection Bay is always navigable. Seward sits at the foot of Mount Marathon, the site of a world famous foot race. On July 4th people from all over the globe congregate in Seward in order to run up and down the mountain. Rain or shine, cold on sunny weather notwithstanding, hundreds of people vie to be the winner for the current year.

It was at Seward that our southbound journey on *the Baranof* began. When we arrived that cloudy morning, I was enthralled by Seward and its beauty. There our ship sat in the bay, gently rocking with the tide and just waiting for us to board. By today's standards, *the Baranof* would be considered no more than a small cargo ship, but to a little nine-year-old girl, it was a floating palace. In Seward we were met by another cadre of Alaskan friends who came to the dock to say "good bye" one more time. All of this saying "good bye" was becoming exhausting, and Jason and I were anxious and antsy to board the boat.

Finally, when our last "good byes" were said, Dad presented our tickets to the purser, and we were invited to board. Boarding a cruise ship these days is an event; professional photographers snap departure photos, refreshments are served and hostesses are available to assist cruisers at their every turn. Not so in 1952. A gang plank spanned the water from the dock to the ship, and that was it. Dad showed the tickets on the wharf, and we walked across the plank onto the ship. It was just that simple. To Jason and me, though, the ship was opulent. Dad and Mom showed us our small cabins, and then let Jason and me explore the ship.

Compared to today's elegant and gigantic cruise ships, there wasn't much to see, but we didn't know it. Our ship was grand. There was an elegant seating area near the purser's desk that had plush velvet overstuffed chairs and ottomans; there were our cute little cabins; and there was a magnificent dining room. Jason and I explored all the decks with their polished wood railings and canvas deck chairs. On the top deck of *the Baranof,* we ran around the smoke stacks and peered down into the cargo hold.

After all of our exploring, Jason and I stood on the promenade deck with Mother and Dad and took it all in. Sammy was dressed up in a little sailor suit that Mother purchased especially for this trip, and he caught the attention of most of the other passengers. We watched longshoremen manipulate large cranes that lifted giant packing crates, cars, trucks, even live stock, and swung it all down into the boat's hold. Five years earlier, this same boat transported our new Hudson from Seattle to Alaska. Our family had come full circle; it was our turn to travel on *the Baranof.*

Early Alaskan cruises were quite unlike modern cruises, yet the scenery is the same. Our trip to Seattle and our life aboard *the Baranof* lasted one glorious week. There were no scheduled ports-of-call with high-priced land excursions. This failed to dampen our enthusiasm or keep us from enjoying the trip—me that is. Poor Jason! In quick order, he discovered that he didn't have good sea legs. While I thoroughly lavished in every moment of the entire week, Jason spent over half the journey sick in bed. I felt sorry for him, but that didn't stop me from having a good time. Our 1952 cruise was a blast to this adventuresome nine-year-old.

The first two cruise days were in the open seas of the Gulf of Alaska, and that's where Jason seemed to be the sickest. Eventually, we entered the drop-dead gorgeous Alaskan Inside Passage. Our little ship was small enough to negotiate the beautiful Wrangell

Narrows—one of Alaska's most breathtaking waterways. In those narrows we visited Petersburg (Alaska's "little Norway") and Wrangell, but we didn't stop at either port long enough to disembark. Our only scheduled disembarkation of the entire week was at Sitka, the old Russian capital of Alaska.

Like a precious jewel, Sitka rests on the western shores of Baranof Island. Across the waterway is Mt. Edgecombe, a dormant volcanic island. What a glorious day we had in Sitka. It was a Sunday; nothing was open, but the five of us tromped all over that historic little town nevertheless. We worshipped together at the world famous St. Michael's Cathedral that dominates the city of Sitka even today. It was a typical Russian Orthodox service; while the priest chanted, men and boys stood on one side of the church and women and girls stood on the other side.

We climbed Castle Hill where the Russian flag was lowered in 1867 for the last time and replaced with the stars and stripes. We walked through the forests and admired skillfully carved and beautifully crafted Native American totem poles. Alaskan native women sat cross-legged by the ship with their handcrafts displayed on blankets before them. We chatted with these people and looked at their wares, but since it was Sunday, Dad didn't buy anything. Our day in Sitka was my ninth birthday, and it was a fabulous day.

There was only one other stop on our 1952 cruise—Juneau, Alaska's capital. The night before our visit to Juneau, the captain informed the passengers that we would be in and out of Juneau before dawn, but we would still have time to disembark if we chose. Most of the passengers opted to sleep through this early visit. No businesses would be open between 4:00 AM and 8:00 AM, and it would still be semi-dark. Mother, Dad, and I, though, were adventuresome and wanted to see Juneau. Dad set the alarm for 4:00 AM; and at that early hour, the three of us left the ship to explore Juneau. Jason stayed behind on *the Baranof* to watch Sammy.

There were a few people loading and unloading cargo at the dock, but Juneau was still asleep that early May morning. That didn't daunt us one bit. Mother and Dad and I meandered down Franklin Street past the famed Red Dog Saloon, closed and quiet in the wee morning hours after another night's drinking and partying. Together we climbed steep streets until we reached the territorial capital building with its office buildings across the street. Around the corner from the capital, we took a quick glance at the Governor's Mansion, but didn't go down to see it. We wandered around until we discovered the grade school and high school situated side by side on Fifth Street. One block in the opposite direction from the school, we took a quick glance toward St. Nicholas Russian Orthodox Church, the oldest church in Juneau, and famous for its octagonal shape. We even peered up the mountain past Seventh Street into the wilderness beyond where just seventy years earlier gold had been discovered in "them thar hills."

Reluctantly, we re-boarded *the Baranof.* Unspoken among the three of us was the knowledge that with this brief visit to Juneau, we were saying "good bye" to Alaska forever. Our stop in Juneau was the end of our Alaskan experience, or at least that's what we thought in May of 1952.

Little did we know what the next year would bring and that in just a mere fifteen months, we would be back "home" in Alaska. Little did we know that the school we saw shrouded in semi-darkness that May morning would be my school one year later, and that each day I would walk past that famous little church on my way to and from school. Little did we know that one day soon we would actually live on Seventh Street near the old gold mine trails. And, little did we know that Mother would one day work in the office building across the street from the territorial capital or that she would come perilously close to losing her life in that very building. Alaska was history, we thought. We didn't fully realize it in May 1952, but Alaska had its hold on us, and we would be back.

In May of 1952, though, our family had other things on our minds. We were headed south to Seattle to take delivery of our new car—a 1952 Chevy coupe. Mother and Dad planned to visit family in Washington and Oregon, attend a big church convention in Kansas City, go to Oklahoma to visit family, and then make the journey across the United States to our new home in Ohio. Major adventures and entirely new horizons lay before us all. We kids had no idea of the magnitude of it all, and I doubt that Mom and Dad did either.

Chapter 3
The Summer of 1952

On our final morning on *the Baranof,* we were awakened by the dining room steward calling us to breakfast. After a week aboard, we were accustomed to him going up and down the halls with a handheld xylophone on which he tapped a tune inviting us to the next meal. This day, however, was uniquely different than any of the other six days. As the steward came down the hall with his xylophone, he tapped his customary little tune and added this final invitation: "Breakfast is now being served. Eat it and beat it!"

That was it. We ate our last shipboard breakfast and then disembarked into the big city of Seattle. What a difference Seattle was from Fairbanks, or even Anchorage for that matter. Seattle seemed HUGE to me, and it was big to Mother and Dad as well. In Alaska we didn't even know what traffic was; Seattle was full of traffic—especially Boeing Aircraft traffic just south of Seattle on old Highway 99. Everyone in the Northwest, it appeared, seemed to be heading either North or South on Highway 99—the only main traffic artery at that time in the entire region. Seattle and its roads were a culture shock to all five of us—especially Dad.

In December 1949 our family flew to Seattle and took delivery of a brand new Ford "Woody." That was a dilly of a car, and it was ours to drive as long as Dad pastored the Fairbanks mission, but it belonged to the church. The first task, then, that Dad had to do when we arrived in Seattle in 1952 was take delivery of our new Chevrolet coupe. After we collected our luggage at the Seattle pier, Dad hired a cab and off we went to the Chevrolet dealership. Alaska has car dealerships in nearly every town today, but in 1952 there were few to none.

Seattle's size was overwhelming. Just one year before we left Fairbanks, in 1951, we all celebrated the opening of a brand new office building that had four stories! Now, we found ourselves winding through the streets of Seattle, seeing countless tall buildings, going up and down hills, hearing cars honk, and seeing busses and street cars in abundance. We were definitely in a different world; there was no doubt about it. Soon we arrived at the dealership, and there stood another new car with our name on it.

Our move in 1952 was an expensive one. Mother worked the entire year of 1951-1952 in order to provide funds for the purchase of new furniture for our new home on the outside. In addition, she set aside funds for our luxurious trip south on *the Baranof.* It went without saying that a trip of such opulence demanded new clothes; so she bought those as well. Mother's job was a good one, but adding a new car to all the other purchases restricted the cost of the vehicle that Mother and Dad could afford.

When we left Texas in 1947, Dad purchased a 1946 Hudson Commodore, and it was in the Hudson that we traveled from Texas to Seattle. The Hudson was huge! It had enough room for an army. Our 1949 Ford "Woody" had an abundance of room as well. There was ample room for the three of us kids to spread out on the interminable trek from Texas back to Alaska. Our trip across the American Midwest and up the Alcan Highway in February of 1950 was one of epic proportions, and one that none of us will ever forget. If we hadn't had such a roomy vehicle, we might have all gone crazy on the treacherous 4,000 mile journey.

1946 Hudson

1950 Woody

In the spring of 1952 our family was in an entirely different predicament. Mother and Dad had money to buy a new car, but all they could afford was a small two door 1952 Chevrolet Coupe. After driving first the over-sized Hudson and then the roomy three door station wagon, the Chevy seemed like a Volkswagen Beetle. We were cramped and we were trapped. That little '52 coupe ended up being our family's only form of transportation for the next four years, and ultimately it, too, took us thousands of miles together. I think we were all glad to get rid of it in the end, but for the time being it was all we had.

By the time all the final paper work and bank transactions were completed, our first day in Seattle was nearly over. The relaxing days aboard *the Baranof* quickly became a distant memory. Mother had two aunts who lived south of Seattle near Longview, and it was our

1952 Chevy Coupe

goal to drive approximately one-hundred miles that day and spend our first night back in the states with one of them. It was roughly 5:00 P.M. when Dad drove out of the Seattle dealership and headed south on Highway 99. We were instantly engulfed in Boeing Aircraft shift change traffic, and Dad was in traffic shock. It seemed to me that we waited an eternity just to merge into the traffic. Finally, Dad found an opening and maneuvered the little coupe into the never ending stream of southbound traffic. We were unquestionably in a different world.

And what a beautiful world it was. The great U. S. Northwest seemed to be just an extension of the Alaskan beauty that we had grown to love. Late that evening, Dad survived the incessant traffic, and we eventually arrived in Longview at Mother's aunt's house. Flowers are prolific in the Northwest, and my aunt had one of the most gorgeous rose gardens I've ever seen—even to this day. Mother's aunt had no children of her own; Mother was her namesake, so she was doubly glad to see Mother and all of us.

After a day or two in the Longview/Kelso area visiting both of Mother's aunts, we squeezed into the car again—cramped as usual—and headed south toward Southern Oregon. Our next stop was to be in Medford to visit Gramma and Mother's sister and brother.

Our trip to Medford was a continuation of Highway 99. We passed beautiful Mt. St. Helen's with its spectacular reflection in Spirit Lake. Nearly thirty-four years later to the day, that same mountain made world history when it blew its top one May morning. In 1952, though, Mt. St. Helen's and Spirit Lake were a beautiful, placid, and breathtaking spectacle.

The Columbia River divides Washington and Oregon, and when Dad crossed the bridge, we were once again in major city traffic; this time it was Portland, Oregon. Today, freeways are cleverly engineered with clover leafs, entry and exit ramps, and city by-passes. In 1952, however, highways ran through the middle of every town, village, or city along their paths. Portland's many stoplights and turns and twists were major for Dad. Eventually, he made it through the city, but Portland traffic was just another example of stateside traffic frustration.

Medford is just a few miles north of the California border, with only Ashland, Oregon separating it from California. Dad drove and drove that day; he drove through Salem, Albany, Eugene, Roseburg, Grants Pass, and a dozen other smaller places. Each town or village forced us to slow to a crawl and stop at every stop sign, stop light, or blinking light. If we were confronted with road construction, we didn't just slow down like drivers do today. Absolutely not! We stopped; sometimes for a few minutes, but occasionally for an hour. This starting and stopping was a customary part of the driving experience before President Eisenhower inaugurated the Interstate freeway system. Dad drove nearly 400 miles between my aunt's house in Longview and Gramma's house in Medford. It was a tedious and exhausting drive.

Dad's mother died before I was born, and Mother's father died when she was two, so I never knew those two grandparents. Dad's father lived in Oklahoma, and although I knew him, my mother's mom—my Gramma—was the grandparent that I truly knew. She was a remarkable woman, and I loved being with her. Life dealt her several severe blows that could have crushed an ordinary person, but not my grandmother. Despite the loss of two husbands to premature deaths and astronomic Depression Era setbacks, she maintained a love for life and an optimist outlook. She took joy in playing tricks, staying up late, or playing her guitar and singing old ballads. Jason and I always eagerly anticipated being with her.

When her second husband died and left her with a young teen-age son, Gramma packed everything she owned into a little car and headed west from Oklahoma to be near Mother's sister in Oregon. Now, all of Mother's immediate family lived in Medford. Gramma's house was extremely modest, but we looked forward to our visits with her with great expectations. Our eagerness to see all our Medford relatives made the drive between Longview and Medford seem even longer. At long last we arrived, and what a reunion we had. The last time we were with our Oregon relatives, little Sammy was barely two years old, and I was only in the first grade. Now, Sammy was ready for kindergarten, Jason was going into the seventh grade, and I was a grown-up fourth grader.

In 1947 Gramma was upset that we were moving to Alaska and would be so far away from her. In 1952, she was upset again. To Gramma, Ohio seemed as far removed from the West Coast as Alaska. In truth, it nearly was. One more time we were moving thousands of miles away from family and friends. And once again, we were headed to a brand new part of the country—one that none of us knew much about. Mom and Dad always loved an adventure; they were excited, and we were excited, also. Our Medford stay was all too short. Just a day or two after we arrived, we crammed into the little coupe and again headed south for California. Mother and Dad wanted to get to Kansas City by mid-June to attend a large church convention so we had to hurry.

Mother and Dad always took advantage of their moves to introduce us to America's abundant beauty and diversity. When we came south for Christmas in 1949, our time was limited. In 1952, though, Dad wasn't scheduled to begin his new job until the beginning of August. So, in that summer, we were able to see much more of the continental United States. Leaving Medford, we crossed the California border and drove past beautiful Lake Shasta and Mount Lassen Volcanic Park in Northern California. Although this 10,500 foot peak paled in comparison to many of Alaska's mountains, we still enjoyed learning about it. In the mid-1800s Mt. Lassen's height was a prominent landmark for westward California travelers. I could only imagine what it must have been like to see this active volcano from a covered wagon way back in California's pioneer days.

In Sacramento, we stopped to visit some of Mother and Dad's friends and enjoyed the warm California sunshine and outdoor air. Summers in Alaska are spectacular, but nothing compared to the warmth of the California sunshine. And so, our trip continued through Central California, over the Grape Vine, and into Southern California where once again Dad fought traffic on California's many freeways. Once we left Southern California, we headed east across Arizona and New Mexico.

In 1949 when we came outside for Christmas, Jason and I saw television for the very first time. In some now forgotten California home, we watched *the Hopalong Cassidy* show. We were captivated. When we returned to Alaska in 1950 after our epic Christmas trip, Jason and I both remembered the excitement of that old black and white TV western. Since there was no television anywhere in Alaska then, we were two of the few Alaskan children who had even seen TV. Our brief 1948 encounter with TV became an exaggerated memory for both of us.

In 1952 about half the people we visited had a TV in their living room. This was absolutely too good to be true. Dad always coupled Alaska missionary programs in local churches with our trips outside. Each night our family was hosted in the home of a pastor or someone in his congregation. Jason and I didn't care what the house was like or who the people were, we just hoped that our host of the day owned a TV and that we would be allowed to watch a program or two. Sometimes we were lucky. It was on this trip that we were introduced to *Roy Rogers and Dale Evans*, the *Three Stooges*, *George Burns and Gracie Allen*, and *Captain Kangaroo*. The world was modernizing, and we were now a part of it.

During the first part of our 1952 trip, we were on a tight schedule because of the church convention in Kansas City. This made our trip through California and across the American Southwest hurried. We still took time to visit Joshua Tree National Monument and the Grand Canyon. All too soon, we were back in West Texas at Aunt Ruth's ranch, and again Mom and Dad left the three of us there while they went on to the convention. We stayed on the ranch in the winter of 1949 while they went to Kansas City, so we knew it pretty well. In December the ranch was chilly and windy, but in June it was down right hot and dusty.

Aunt Ruth's ranch was just as remote and just as removed from Alaska as it had been two years earlier. Everything on the ranch seemed frozen in time. There was certainly no TV; there wasn't even indoor plumbing. Aunt Ruth still made huge farm breakfasts of biscuits and gravy and eggs and sausage and fresh sliced tomatoes each morning. She still fed the chickens and separated the milk from the cream, and the horses still came up to the salt lick by the horse trough to get water and salt. It was lonely and a bit boring for all three of us on the ranch after exotic California and the Grand Canyon. And, of course, we missed television; yet, there was plenty of room to run and play.

We spent a restless week on the ranch waiting for Mother and Dad to return so we could continue our eastward adventure. Aunt Ruth's ranch was twenty miles from the closest town, a town of less than 2,000 people. Those twenty miles were all dusty dirt roads, but after five years in Alaska, we knew all about dusty dirt roads. One day Aunt Ruth loaded us into her pickup and took us to town. Her little West Texas town had a general store that sold just about anything you needed, but not necessarily everything you wanted. Dad thought that jeans were unladylike, but Aunt Ruth decided it was okay for me to wear jeans while I was on the ranch. Consequently, it was in the summer of 1952 that I had my first pair of jeans. I thought jeans made me look like one of the western women that Jason and I had seen on TV, and that thrilled me.

When Mother and Dad returned from the convention, we drove to Elk City in Western Oklahoma. Elk City was Mom and Dad's home town; it was the place they met and where both of them went to school their entire lives. They each had many relatives there. We spent another week in that area visiting my grandfather, uncles and aunts, and dozens of cousins. Some of the family lived in town, and some lived on farms outside town. They were all pleased to see us.

When we went to Alaska in 1947 everyone in Elk City thought my parents had lost their minds and that we wouldn't survive the cold or the remoteness. Now in 1952, our healthy family disproved their skepticism, and everyone was resigned to the fact that Dad was determined to follow his dream and serve wherever He felt God wanted him to go. Our Oklahoma family, though, still shared the same feelings as Mom's Oregon family. They simply didn't understand why Dad kept moving us so far away from everyone. It didn't seem odd to Jason and me, though. In Alaska many adults had adopted us as their grandchildren and extended family, so we just assumed that people in Ohio would do the same.

When we left Elk City that June of 1952, all five of us were on a brand new journey. Dad and Mom drove eastward across Oklahoma toward Arkansas. Dad was born in eastern Oklahoma out in the middle of no place in a region called Owl Creek. That little area no longer exists; it's simply not on the map, and it's only a vague memory to the few older locals remaining. Our 1952 trip resurrected a lot of nostalgic memories that Dad shared with us. One specific story absolutely astounded Jason and me:

In 1923 when Dad was only six years old, his family moved in a covered wagon across the state of Oklahoma from Owl Creek in the southeast to Elk City in the west. Jason had studied about the Oregon Trail in school, and Dad had read us stories about it on our long winter nights in Fairbanks, but I just couldn't believe that my own father traveled in a covered wagon. Wow! My Dad was a *real* pioneer. Dad told us that he and his older brother sat on the back of the wagon and counted cars. In 1923 it took a full week to travel approximately three hundred miles across the state. During that one week, Dad and his brother counted five hundred cars. In 1952, we could see five hundred cars in a glance, but in 1923 there were so few cars that it took an entire week to count five hundred. Times had changed; that was apparent.

We stopped for a few days in Arkansas to visit two of Dad's friends from college. One lived in Little Rock and pastored a large church that had a radio program. Dad presented one of his Alaska services at that church and spoke on the radio while we stayed in the home of his friends. These people had a girl my age, and the two of us had fun playing together. The friendship we forged in 1952 lasted into adulthood until she passed away in 2005.

After a couple days in Little Rock, we headed to Jonesboro to visit one of Mother's favorite friends. This lady and mother were college roommates, and she was married to a pastor who was also one of Dad's friends. This man was one of the most interesting individuals I have ever known. He was born blind, but his blindness hadn't stopped him from attaining a college education and following his heart. He did his studying from a Braille Bible, and his wife did the driving, etc. Together they were a remarkable couple. They had a daughter Jason's age and a son my age. When we left, Dad's friend told him that his Alaska service was one of the best he had ever "seen." He didn't think of himself as blind, so no one else considered him handicapped either.

Dad had been to Arkansas once or twice, but when we left Arkansas in late June of 1952, our whole family was in uncharted territory. Jason and I had read about the early settlers who moved westward across the United States, first settling Ohio and the Midwest and ultimately going on to the West Coast. Our family had certainly gone west and ventured into the wilderness in 1947 when we moved to Alaska, *the Last Frontier.* Now our family was moving in the exact opposite direction from the early westward expansion. We were moving east.

Chapter 4
Traveling Eastward

Once we left Arkansas in our little Chevy Coupe that summer of 1952, our family was in brand new territory. Thousands and thousands of Americans call the region east of the Mississippi River their home, but no one that we knew lived in the East. In a sense, the area where we were moving in 1952 was just as remote to us as Alaska was in 1947. Mother and Dad lived in Oklahoma all their lives until they married and moved to Texas. Our lives changed dramatically in 1947 when we moved to Alaska, and this move in 1952 was no less dramatic.

Even though Mother was born in Oklahoma, she had roots in the east. Her natural father who died when she was two years old was from New York State. Now that she had an opportunity, Mother was determined to connect with her father's family—one that she had never known. My mother's father was a German immigrant who entered the United States like thousands of other Europeans through Ellis Island in the New York harbor. His family were staunch Roman

Catholics who finally settled in Upstate New York. When his mother died shortly after the family settled, the children were split up and parceled out to various agencies and families around the country.

My future grandfather, who was a strapping young teenager by then, was sent to the Midwest to work on the farm of a very strict German speaking family. They had no love for this young boy who was placed in their care, rather they saw him as free labor and were abusive and unkind to him. As family legend goes, my maternal grandfather took all of this abuse he could stand. One day he ran away straight to the United States Army recruiting office. He was underage for recruitment, but he was so desperate to get away from his unbearable surroundings that he lied about his age in order to join the army.

Whether the recruiter believed him, or whether he just took pity on him, no one ever really knew, but at the age of sixteen, Mother's father enlisted into the United States Army. He was a good looking and hard working German lad who did well and quickly made his way upwards through the ranks. The Army was impressed with his people skills and likeable ways, and after stints in Key West in Florida and Fort Vancouver in Washington State, he was stationed in Oklahoma as a recruiting officer.

My grandmother came from a large Kentucky family—the Music clan. Like many others, the Musics migrated to Oklahoma in covered wagons at the time of the great Land Run. They were too late for the "good" land in Eastern Oklahoma, but they were still able to homestead in Western Oklahoma's Indian Territory. There were eight children in Gramma's family, a family divided into two different age groups of children; four adult children and four young girls. Two of the older four were already married with children of their own, but they joined the family caravan just the same. My grandmother was the second oldest of the four young girls. When her family moved to Indian Territory, Gramma fell in love with Oklahoma.

Gramma's entire family ultimately settled near the little western Oklahoma town of Elk City. Gramma's father and her married brothers all homesteaded and farmed near one another. Gramma was fun loving and talented; she was extremely musical; she was a good painter and artist; she wrote poetry; and she was an excellent story teller. In a word, she was an amazing individual. She planned to finish school and attend college. Those were lofty goals for anyone in the early 1900s, especially for a woman. But fate wasn't in her favor.

Grandmother's father came in from the field one day for lunch, laid down for an after dinner nap, and died. By this time two of Gramma's sisters were married. So, at the age of eighteen, Gramma found herself in charge of the farm. Shortly after her father's death, one of her sisters-in-laws died in child birth—leaving twins. Both infants soon died, and Gramma's brother was so heartbroken that he left Oklahoma and his older children behind and moved as far away as he could—to the new State of Washington. Gramma was now responsible both for the farm and for her brother's surviving children.

By 1916, the extended family absorbed some of Gramma's many responsibilities, and she was able to pursue her dream of a college education. She moved a few miles away from Elk City to the little town of El Reno, and enrolled in Oklahoma State Teacher's College. To support herself while attending college, Gramma took a job at a small local hotel working as a maid and cook. It was at that little hotel that my grandmother and grandfather met. It was love at first sight.

Dreams of a college education were put on the back burner when Gramma married the man of her dreams. No two people could ever have come from more different worlds. Gramma was from Oklahoma and had always been a part of a large extended, fun-loving family. She literally had dozens of aunts and uncles, cousins, and sisters and brothers. The Music clan had huge get-togethers, shared a love for pranks and wholesome good fun, and true to their name—they loved to sing. "Singing schools" were all the rage then, and Gramma and several others of the Musics attended the Stamps Baxter schools and became experts in reading the old shaped notes. They attended church regularly and were God-fearing, religious people. Everyone in the area knew Gramma and the many Musics, and everyone loved them.

My grandfather, on the other hand, was from an entirely different world. After his family immigrated to America and his mother died, he virtually had no family. He remembered one sister with fondness, but beyond that he held a disdain for his own family after the way he was treated when his mother died. For all practical explanations, he was a young man totally alone in the world. And yet, the marriage worked. Gramma and her new young husband from New York were deliriously happy together. He was stationed in several little Oklahoma towns as a recruiter, and during the first five years of their marriage, both my mother's older sister and my mother were born. They were a happy foursome.

When my mother was a toddler, my grandfather was transferred to Fort Sam Houston near San Antonio, Texas. Gramma still held her dream of a college education, and she hoped that one day when her two little girls were older, she would be able to finish school. But that, too, wasn't meant to be. When Mother was two years old and her sister was four, their father died unexpectedly. Gramma's dreams of an education were shattered for a lifetime. She packed up her two little girls and moved back to Oklahoma with a determination to raise them in the loving arms of her large extended family. And that's exactly how it happened. My mother and her sister had a glorious childhood during the Depression in Oklahoma. They didn't have much, but they were surrounded by family, friends, and fun. It was a good childhood.

And yet, to my mother there was always a missing piece. My grandmother and grandfather were married such a few short years that at his death Gramma hadn't yet had a chance to meet his sister in New York. Life had forever altered any thought of such a meeting for Gramma, and now in 1952 over thirty years had passed since the death of my mother's father. Since Mother had always dreamed of meeting her New York cousins and her aunt, moving to Ohio in the summer of 1952 provided the perfect opportunity for such a meeting. It was a lifetime dream fulfilled for Mother, and I got to go along for the ride.

And what a ride it was. When we left Arkansas, we traveled to Memphis, Tennessee. From there Dad crossed the state of Tennessee in a diagonal fashion which took us through Tennessee's capital— Nashville. We all remembered the rugged and grueling trip of 1949 and the infamous trip up the Alcan Highway in February 1950 *(See Little House in the Arctic, Chapter 10)*. Somehow we had the idea that the roads in the eastern part of the U.S. would be more modern and easier to travel. Part of Dwight Eisenhower's 1952 presidential election promise was to construct an interstate highway system, but in June of 1952 Eisenhower hadn't been elected yet, and America's roads were rugged at best and primitive in many places.

One of the many things that made highway travel so rugged in the 1950s was the lack of decent roadside housing. Today, there are hotel and motel chains in every city and town that offer housing to match any pocketbook. Modern travelers can make advance reservations on the phone or the Internet. Not so in 1952. I have frightening recollections of some of the places we stayed on our journey to New York. Usually, we stayed in a locally owned motel along the way; cleanliness, safety, and amenities of these places varied from town to town.

Dad never took a room until he checked it out; that was a given. If the room didn't seem clean or safe, we drove on until he found a suitable lodging spot for the night. In some places Dad couldn't even find a motel. In those towns he looked for private homes that had signs in the yard indicating "Rooms for Rent." These places were the most foreboding of all. Sometimes they were adequate, and sometimes they weren't. No one even dreamed of planning ahead and making reservations; you just drove until you found a bed, or you drove all night. Regardless, each night Dad was able to find some spot that was relatively safe, and we survived our eastward trek.

In addition to the challenge of finding decent housing along the highway, roadside food was another travel adventure of the 1950s. It wasn't until we finally reached Pennsylvania that we discovered the first chain restaurant any of us had ever heard about—Howard Johnson's. In the meantime, we followed a similar "search and find" routine when it came to eating. Dad would check out a little café or coffee shop. If it looked clean, and if he thought he could afford the prices, we parked the car and went it. Air-conditioning was a new extravagance in the early '50s; few restaurants and public places were refrigerated, and virtually no cars had air-conditioning. Consequently, most of our meals were eaten in stuffy, hot "Mom and Pop" establishments where we often suffocated under ceiling or window fans while we tried to eat a hamburger or a sandwich.

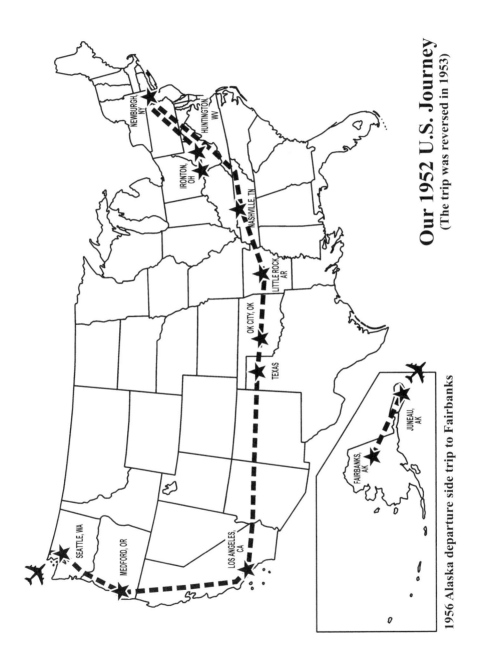

Our 1952 U.S. Journey
(The trip was reversed in 1953)

1956 Alaska departure side trip to Fairbanks

It's impossible to talk about U. S. travel in the '50s without mentioning gas stations and their restrooms. Perhaps that was the biggest challenge of all. There were chain gas companies then, but their standards were few. To use the restroom, you usually had to request a key. We never were certain why. Even the few restrooms that had signs indicating that they were checked periodically for cleanliness left a lot to be desired. More than once I remember holding my breath, getting my business done, and rushing back outside for some fresh air.

Today, most states have lovely state operated rest stops where coffee is served and vending machines are accessible. The only refreshments available at the 1950s gas stations were pop and candy from vending machines. Pop was a luxury for us, and Mom and Dad seldom bought us any snack food or candy between meals. Every once in a while, they treated us to a Hershey bar, but usually we just drove and drove and then drove some more without any breaks or refreshments.

We thought the roads in Arkansas and Tennessee were rugged, but we had no idea what rugged was until we began to drive through the hills of Eastern Kentucky. Kentucky is a beautiful state with gorgeous rolling hills. It has many lovely people, but in 1952 the part we saw was pretty backwoods. We had heard and read about hillbillies; on this trip, we saw them—and more than once. Perhaps we saw so many hillbillies because we got caught in some monstrous detours and ultimately were lost for several hours.

Driving though Kentucky in 1952 was most assuredly a memorable experience. One or two of our detours took us far back into the hill country where we drove past houses so primitive that they made the sourdough cabins of Alaska look modern. Maybe it was because it was so different from Alaska that all five of us were speechless. Entire families lined up on their porches and gawked at us as if they had never seen a car before that day. Our family in the new little coupe was indeed a novelty as we drove up and down hoots and hollers that had names we couldn't even pronounce. It was a cultural experience to say the least.

PHOTO ALBUM

◄ *Alaska's Flag*
(See Appendix
Number 1)

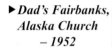 ► *Dad's Fairbanks,*
Alaska Church
– 1952

▲ *Dad's Ironton, Ohio Church – 1953*

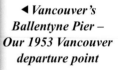

▲ Princess Louise –
Our 1953 Cruiseship

◄ Vancouver's
Ballentyne Pier –
Our 1953 Vancouver
departure point

► Old Juneau/
Douglas Bridge
– 1950s

◄ Juneau
– 1950s

►Juneau
Waterfront
– 1950s

▲Juneau Harbor as seen from Douglas Island today

◀ *Present day Mt. Roberts Tram*

▶ *A Juneau street descending Mt. Roberts*

▼ *Juneau from the top of Mt. Roberts today*

◄ Present remains of Juneau Mines

► Mine remains as seen from Juneau's pier (beneath Mt. Roberts Tram)

▲ Dad's boss, Dr. Powers, at the Juneau Airport – 1954

▲ *Juneau House – the "fixer-upper"*

◄ *Juneau House – after a major face lift*

► *My Fifth Grade Teacher, Miss Hermes – 2003*

◄ *Mendenhall Glacier – 1954 Site of present parking lot*

► *Mendenhall as it appears today*

◄ *My brothers and I on Mendenhall Glacier – 1954*

► *Nugget Falls at Mendenhall – Visible today, but covered with ice in the '50s*

*◄ Mendenhall Glacier
from Auk Bay*

STATE OF ALASKA
DEPARTMENT OF HEALTH
&
SOCIAL SERVICES

*◄ Territorial
Office Building
where the
murder occurred*

*► Governor's
Mansion*

◀1950's Juneau Library – Present Day Museum

▲ The OOLA that my Mother and I rode to Douglas Ski Bowl

▶ Whale watching near Juneau

◄ *Juneau's Russian Orthodox Church*

▲ *4th of July Parade – 1954*

▲ *Whitter Tunnel: Both cars and trains use the same passageway*

▲ *Whittier Tunnel: Mt. Maynard one way tunnel entrance*

◄ *Whittier: Simon Buckner Building. The entire city lived and worked in this one building*

◀ *My brothers and I at the Pioneer Statue in Sitka – 1952*

▲ *Piano in Skagway that the "Alaskan Flag" song was composed on (See Apendix Number 2)*

◀ *Original Ketchikan Sign*

◀ *Modern Ketchikan Sign*

Creek Street – Ketchikan ▶

▲ *Saxman Village Totem Park – Ketchikan*

◀ *Mt. McKinley – called Denali (The Great One) by Alaskans*

Chapter 5
A Side Trip to New York

After wandering through the hills of Eastern Kentucky for two or three memorable days, we crossed the state border and entered West Virginia. Daily, in Kentucky we searched for adequate housing and were forced to eat in a conglomeration of eateries that were as strange to us as the vicinity. We thought West Virginia would be different, but there was no difference between the two states. We continued to roam and ramble up and down hoots and hollers and endless detours. We were determined, though, to persevere on to New York to meet Mother's family—the family that she had never met in her entire life.

At last we crossed into the State of Pennsylvania. Mother and Dad studied and prepared for this trip before we left Alaska, and throughout the entire incessant journey, they had been telling us about the new modern highway in Pennsylvania. We hoped they were right, and we all waited with bated breath. We weren't disappointed. On our journey down the West Coast of the United States in 1949 and earlier in June of 1952, we drove on four lane highways in Southern

California, but we certainly hadn't seen any four lane highways on this trip since we left the Turner Turnpike in Eastern Oklahoma.

The Pennsylvania Turnpike was constructed before World War II, and it was a modern marvel for its era. Every single mile of highway was four lanes, which was terrific. But, this modern turnpike had more amenities than any highway we had ever seen. It was a toll road, and other than our previous brief encounter with the Turner Turnpike, I had never heard of a toll road. Dad explained to me that toll roads and bridges have nominal fees that eventually pay for the upkeep and construction costs. I soon learned that toll roads weren't new. There were toll roads in the East long before the West was ever explored and long before paved roads and cars were even a thought.

This modern turnpike was fabulous. Tunnels blasted through the mountains created smooth, curving roads rather than steep inclines and sharp curves. The entire length of the turnpike had lovely manicured shoulders. The things, though, that fascinated and delighted us most of all were the accommodations. Every few miles, there was a center median that could be approached from either direction. In these medians were the first chain restaurants and gas station combinations we had ever seen. Today chain restaurants are abundant, but in 1952, they were a new concept and absolutely refreshing to weary travelers like us.

In the beautifully landscaped medians, there was always a Howard Johnson's restaurant and a modern, CLEAN gas station. Sometimes there was even a Howard Johnson's Motor Lodge. We never stayed in one of those lodges because my parents thought they were too expensive, but we did eat at the restaurants. They were clean, modern, and air-conditioned. The floors were carpeted, the booths were padded, and the waitresses wore attractive, clean starched uniforms. The menus were predictable, and the food was well prepared, sanitary, and good. The thing that we liked most, though, was Howard Johnson's many different ice cream flavors.

Once or twice, Dad treated us to an ice cream cone at a Howard Johnson's gas station: one scoop, five cents; two scoops, ten cents! Dad only purchased five cent scoops, but we didn't care. Just to be a part of this modern travel setting was exciting enough. Mother and Dad enjoyed the ice cream treats and the change from our grueling travel experiences as much as we did. It was the 1950s, and there was something magical about this progressive highway. How different it was from the way things had been just five years earlier when we drove westward across the U. S. in the new Hudson. Dad did the majority of the driving—hundreds and hundreds of endless miles of rough roads—so this change to an advanced modern highway was a welcome relief to him most of all.

Our trip in 1947 to Seattle from South Texas was pretty much a straight shot across the United States. We only stopped for Dad to hold a mission service or provide a place for Mother to care for Sammy, the new baby. The trip outside in 1949 and 1950 gave Mom and Dad an opportunity to introduce us to some of America's national parks when we visited Yosemite, Grand Canyon, and the Petrified Forest. Now, our 1952 eastern trip was opening brand new doors of national beauty and historic adventure.

One of these experiences occurred along the Pennsylvania Turnpike. The turnpike had an exit to Valley Forge. In 1952 I had just completed third grade so I knew little about American history, but Dad and Jason knew a lot. Valley Forge was the historic winter and spring encampment of George Washington and the Revolutionary

Army. From December 1777 through June 1778, the outnumbered and undersupplied patriots endured hardships beyond my wildest imagination. After five years in Alaska, I understood cold, but in Alaska we were prepared for the cold. These revolutionaries, I learned, were not prepared for such a harsh winter.

With virtually nothing going their way, the colonial troops persevered through snow, bitter cold, inadequate housing, and lack of food. Sadly, many of them perished during the winter of 1778. The British Redcoats were certain that the upstart revolutionaries would eventually fail in their efforts to gain independence from old King George. Little did the British understand the will of the early American patriots' spirit. After one of the worst winters on record, Washington and his troops prevailed. In spring, they rose from their winter hibernation with a vengeance that ultimately ridded the colonies of everything British and established this new nation.

After Dad explained some of this history to me, I was as excited as Jason to visit Valley Forge. What an experience that was. Dad parked our little car, and the five of us walked through the grounds that seemed hallowed by the heroism of the patriots and what they had endured here so that we might enjoy such a marvelous country. In the gift shop, I purchased a miniature Valley Forge cup and saucer that had a picture of George and Martha Washington on it—a souvenir that I kept for years after that. Dad wanted to take us to Gettysburg and allow us another opportunity to visit the famous Civil War battlefield, but time was getting short, and that side trip was shelved for another time.

Instead of visiting Gettysburg, Dad continued driving through Pennsylvania until he turned north toward New York and the city of Newburgh. This city, sixty miles north of New York City on the

Hudson River at the foot of the Catskill Mountains, was the home of Mother's family. Things seemed different to all of us in the East. In the West, and especially in Alaska, everything was relatively new, and people were adventuresome. In the East things were older and more historic. The Catskill Mountains were beautiful, but certainly not as dramatic as the Rocky Mountains of Colorado or Mount McKinley in Alaska.

Even though we didn't have time to visit Gettysburg, Dad did take time for one more side trip. About twenty miles south of Newburgh he turned off the highway and drove to West Point Military Academy. Wow! We were certainly a long way from Fairbanks, Alaska, and what a marvelous trip we were having.

At long last we arrived in Newburgh—which for all of us was a big unknown. Mother's New York family had never met either Mother or her sister. As different as things seemed geographically in the East, there were also extreme differences between Mother's long lost New York family and the Oklahoma family that we all knew and loved. Looking back, I think they were as equally bewildered by the differences as we were. When we arrived in Newburgh, though, everyone seemed genuinely thrilled to meet us. My father was a Protestant minister, and all of Mother's New York family were devout Catholics. They didn't understand us, and we didn't understand them. Regardless of the differences, though, it was a memorable meeting.

Our first stay was with Mother's cousin and his family in Newburgh. They had a daughter my age who taught me how to ride a bicycle. I balanced at the top of a hill on her bike while she steadied it. Then, with me yelling and screaming like a wild banshee, she would give me a shove down the hill. As the bicycle sped wildly and wobbled down the hill, I did my best to begin peddling. It was an insane way to learn to ride a bike, and I took several bad spills before I eventually got the hang of it and began riding on my own. Possibly, self-preservation is what inspired me to learn to ride that bicycle.

Mother's aunt who lived in Kingston, New York was the relative who wanted to meet us the most. She was Mother's father's last living sibling, and she had always hoped and prayed to meet one of her two Oklahoma nieces. Mother's cousin drove us out to the country to meet Aunt Emma, and while Mother, Sammy, and I visited her in the country, Dad took Jason on a two day trip to New York City.

One of Dad's Oklahoma college buddies, and the man who stood up with Dad at my parents' wedding, lived in New York City. Jason was named for this man, and Dad wanted him to spend some time with his namesake. In college, Dad's friend was studying to be a Protestant minister like Dad, but somewhere along the way, he changed his path and became a priest. While he had this opportunity, Dad wanted to visit his friend. When Dad and Jason returned from New York City, they had great stories to tell about their visits to the Empire State Building and St. Patrick's Cathedral. I was envious and knew that one day I, too, would visit New York City. They made us even more wishful when they shared about their side trip to Washington Irving's famous Sleepy Hollow and the land of Rip Van Winkle.

Visiting Mother's aunt was the best part of our New York side trip. She lived in a beautiful white house that sat on a sloping hill with broad lawns that practically went on forever. My new found cousin and I ran up and down those hills while Mother's aunt shared memories with her of the father she never knew. To Mother, this entire trip was a serendipitous opportunity to make connections with a part of her history that she had never known. Mother's aunt cried when she saw me and said that I reminded her of her brother who died so many years before and so many miles away. At first her tears made me sad, but when I saw the joy it brought her to make this connection with her brother's family, I was glad that I looked like my grandfather.

Soon Dad and Jason returned from their soiree to New York City and Sleepy Hollow; we said good byes to the New York relatives and turned the little Chevy southward toward our new home in Ohio. Mother corresponded with these relatives off and on after that, but we never saw any of them again. In truth, we had little in common, but Mother's curiosity and sense of emptiness over the father she never knew were both satisfied. All in all, this side trip was an odd, but meaningful encounter that none of us ever forgot or regretted.

Chapter 6
More Traveling...

Once we completed our side trip to New York and our visit to Mother's long lost relatives, Jason and I thought we would head straight to our new home in Ohio. But Mother and Dad had two more planned stops on this our American odyssey. One of my Mother's Oklahoma cousins and her family lived in the Pittsburg area, so the first stop was to visit the Pennsylvania cousins. Visiting Mother's Oklahoma family was a vast contrast to visiting her New York family.

What a time we had in Pittsburg. Mother and her cousin did a lot of laughing, storytelling, and reminiscing about their childhood days in Oklahoma during the Great Depression. My grandmother and Mother's cousin's mother were sisters; for years they shared everything from holidays to funerals to graduations. Mother's cousin's life in Pittsburg and mother's life in Fairbanks were both far removed from the Dust Bowl era of the 1930s when they were kids together, but that didn't keep them from enjoying each other's company. Mother's cousin had two boys near the ages of Jason and me, so it was fun for us to play with them as well.

Soon this brief reunion came to an end, and we headed to our next destination. Dad and Mother had some college friends who lived in Huntington, West Virginia, so we headed for their home. In Fairbanks we lived in a furnished parsonage with absolutely no furniture of our own. Since shipping furniture to Alaska was so expensive, a furnished parsonage was expedient, and none of us objected. For five years, we were cozy and happy in our *Little House in the Arctic* with its cedar paneled walls and hodge-podge of donated furniture. In 1952, though, Mom and Dad were forced to purchase furniture.

A portion of the money Mother earned our last year in Fairbanks at Pan Am was saved specifically to buy furniture when we moved back to the states. The two cities of Ironton and Huntington are less than a hundred miles apart. Since Huntington is much larger than Ironton, it was the place Mother and Dad chose to purchase an entire house of furniture. We were excited and could hardly wait. How lucky for us; a house full of brand new furniture, a steamship trip, and a new car—all in one summer.

While Mother and Dad shopped for furniture, we visited two different places in West Virginia. Dad's college friend pastored a church in Huntington, and to me his church was huge. We stayed several days in their parsonage next door to the church. This parsonage was a two story brick home with two bathrooms, several bedrooms, and a formal dining room; in addition to all this, they had beautiful furniture. After our humble *Little House in the Arctic*, this house was a palace. I wondered if our new home in Ohio would be this nice or if the furniture that Mom and Dad were buying would be as fancy as theirs. Things were certainly different for pastors in West Virginia than they were for pastors far away in Fairbanks.

During our brief stay in Huntington, I had a brand new experience. Since Dad's friends lived next door to the church; all we had to do was walk across the front lawn to get to church on Sunday morning. This church, though, drove several buses each week to pick up neighborhood children. These buses were merely old school buses that they used to bring children to Sunday school, but I had never ridden on a school bus. In Fairbanks we walked to school each day; I don't even know if they had any school buses when we lived there.

I begged my father and his host to let me ride the Sunday school bus. I think they thought it was humorous, but they agreed and placated me. On Sunday morning I put on my best clothes, walked across the yard, boarded the bus, and road the entire route while they picked up kids for Sunday school. When we finished the route, I was right back where I started—at the church next door to the parsonage. But, I didn't care; I could now say I had been on a school bus. Many years later when I was in high school and had to ride the bus each day, I begged my dad to drive me to school. When I was nine, though, it was a big deal to ride the bus to church.

Our other West Virginia stop was even more unique to me than riding the Sunday school bus. 1952 preceded the days of integration; segregation was a way of life—even in the church. Dad's denomination had a large African American compound and training school in Institute, West Virginia that he wanted to visit. My parents were both very open minded, tolerant, and accepting, and they wanted to meet their African American brothers and sisters and worship with them. The stop in Institute was tremendously memorable for us all; in fact, we made friends there that lasted well into my adult years. The dear people in Institute asked my Dad to present one of his Alaska services, and of course, he obliged. Institute, West Virginia and Fairbanks, Alaska were worlds apart—both geographically and culturally—but the people loved the service, and we truly enjoyed being with them.

When we left West Virginia, we had been on the road nearly six weeks since we left our Oklahoma family. At last, we were headed for our new home in Ironton, Ohio on the Ohio River. Ironton was near a mining area, and its proximity to the river gave the mines a great conduit for transporting ore to the rest of the world. Actually, Ironton is situated in a triangle of cities and states. Within fifty miles there are three cities and three states: Huntington, West Virginia, Ashland, Kentucky, and Ironton, Ohio. When we left Huntington, West Virginia, Dad drove on the Kentucky side of the Ohio River, through Ashland, Kentucky. When we reached the bridge, we crossed the mighty Ohio River to our new home—Ironton, Ohio.

At first blush, Ironton was a disappointment. It was—and still is—a dirty river town. In the late thirties, the old Ohio River had flooded the entire town, so by 1952 there was a massive dike along the river that blocked the view of the river. This dike, though, has saved the areas of Ironton and adjacent Portsmouth more than once since the mighty flood of 1938. Perhaps Ironton was a disappointment because during our journey eastward we had been to so many different places that we began to expect it to be like one of them. Not only was it different than Medford, Elk City, Newburgh, Huntington, and all the other towns and cities we visited that summer, it was completely different from Fairbanks. They were both on rivers, but that seemed to be the only comparison.

Mother and Dad approached this new chapter of our lives with their predictable attitudes of optimism and adventure. They knew that Ironton would be different from Fairbanks, and they encouraged us to embrace those differences and find the good in this new area. We were kids, and we followed their example. All of us, though, were disillusioned by our new parsonage. After staying in the beautiful two story brick parsonage in Huntington, I think we had all secretly hoped for something similar. That was not so.

There were two similarities between the two homes; they were both brick, and they both had two stories. Our new parsonage, however, was old and small. The church was on one corner of the block, and the house stood behind the church on the opposite corner. When the Ohio River flooded in the 1938, our neighbors told us that the former pastor and his family paddled out the upstairs windows of the parsonage into the church next door. Wow! The story seemed far-fetched, but they told it with such assurance, that we believed them.

Our new two story square brick home had three bedrooms upstairs, and a kitchen, dining room, bath, and small living room downstairs. The house had a traditional screened-in front porch that stretched across the front of the house and a small back porch. It had a partial basement that was much different from our basement in Fairbanks. It was more of a cellar—complete with a dirt floor. When our new furniture arrived, and we got it moved in, the house didn't seem too bad. Its one winning feature was that it was a great deal larger than our *Little House in the Arctic.*

While we were initially taken aback by the size and age of the parsonage, the church was not a disappointment at all. It was large, and I thought it was the most beautiful church I had ever seen. Built of red brick, it held an imposing dominance on the corner facing two different streets. As was the custom in those days, our church was built with broad steps that led from the sidewalk to the entrance. When you walked up the stairs, you entered a large foyer that led to the sanctuary.

Dad's church in Ironton, Ohio – 1952

The interior of the church was just as impressive and awe-inspiring as the exterior. The sanctuary seated about four hundred people and had a large platform with imposing pulpit chairs for my father and his guests. There was a great organ, a grand piano, stained glass windows, and a choir loft that seated forty people. Dad's new church even had a balcony. Beneath the sanctuary, there was a full basement with adult meeting rooms. What a difference this magnificent building was compared to our little chapel in Fairbanks. Until I saw this building in Ohio, I thought Dad's church on the corner of Tenth and Noble was pretty awesome, but now I realized how humble our little Alaska church really was.

In addition to the large brick church on the corner and our modest parsonage behind it, the Ironton church owned another building. This building was one block away, and it was lovingly called "The Annex." This annex was the children's Sunday school building, and it was incredible. The Annex was a large frame building that for years was the tabernacle for old fashioned camp meetings. It covered nearly a quarter of a city block, and it was even larger than the church.

It consisted of two distinct sections. The first was the expansive open area that had at one time been used for the summer camp meeting sanctuary; it, too, had a large platform.

On Sunday mornings about two hundred children met in this big open room. We were divided into small groups of approximately ten each, and each of these groups sat around a conglomeration of tables. None of the tables or chairs matched, but Sunday mornings in the tabernacle were magical nevertheless. Music leaders stood on the platform and led us kids in choruses that had accompanying hand motions. Together we sang and sang until it seemed as though we were going to sing the roof right off that old tabernacle.

When the singing was over, each of the small groups of children around the hodge-podge tables had an adult leader who taught that Sunday's lesson. There were no dividers; the noise level was high, but it was a surprisingly effective system. Kids loved it. When Sunday school was over, an adult led each group of children in a caravan to the big brick church on the corner a block away. There, we all sat quietly with our parents during the morning worship service. It was a proud moment for me to sit with my Mom and hear my Daddy preach to this big crowd. Whenever the church wanted to have a big dinner or special occasion, they rearranged the tabernacle, and it doubled as a fellowship hall.

The other part of the tabernacle was entirely different from where we met on Sunday mornings. Behind the platform there were two apartments. In one of these lived a lady named Martha. She was the permanent caretaker for the tabernacle and the church, and with two big buildings located a block apart, she had a full time job. The other apartment was larger than Martha's, and it was kept by the church to house missionaries who were home on furlough. For five years, my family had been called missionaries, and it was definitely a novel idea to know that churches actually provided housing for people home temporarily from distant lands.

A missionary family from Peru was living in the annex apartment during 1952. They had a daughter named Mary Phyllis, who was my age; she became my best friend during our tenure in Ohio. Ironton was her parents' hometown, and this was their year to be in the states on furlough from the jungles along the Amazon River. Dad's church provided the annex apartment for them rent free. Mary Phyllis and I were in the same fourth grade class at the school one block down the street in the opposite direction from the church and the annex.

Even though Mary Phyllis and I were the same age and in the same school class, our lives until 1952 had been diametrically different. She and her two brothers had been romping in shorts and tank tops through South American jungles near the Equator. My two brothers and I, on the other hand, lived near the Arctic Circle where we bundled with layers and layers of clothing nearly every time we stepped out our front door. While they spent time traveling up and down the Amazon River in dugout Indian canoes, we stood on a frozen river near the Arctic Circle and were captivated by the Eskimo Olympics. Both of us had been living on an edge of civilization at one extreme or the other, and now fate brought us together in a river town in southern Ohio.

Soon our new furniture arrived from Huntington, and the few possessions that Mother shipped from Alaska arrived, too. We were definitely traveling light. One night the people in Dad's new church scheduled a big welcome reception for us in the Annex. They knew that we brought little with us but pictures and a few treasured family keepsakes. Several hundred people attended the party, and they went all out to welcome us. It was customary then to give a new pastor a

Ironton Welcome Banquet and Pounding – 1952

"pounding." This idea originated when pastors were totally dependent on their congregations for staple goods. In short, everyone in a congregation brought the pastor and his family a pound of this and a pound of that. The people brought such a pounding that night that Mother didn't need to buy many groceries for several months.

In addition to the dinner and the pounding, we were more overwhelmed when the church presented us with tables full of beautifully wrapped housewarming gifts. Mother said it was like getting married all over again and

Gifts from the Ironton Church

having a giant wedding reception. There were sheets and blankets and towels, kitchen supplies, and dishes and household necessities galore. We came to Ohio with nothing, but these wonderful people made certain that we were set up for housekeeping and normal life back in the lower forty-eight. At last, we were home in our little house and the big church in Ohio, and it was time for this new chapter of our lives to begin in full swing.

Chapter 7
A Year in Ohio

Immediately after the big party in the church annex and even before we were fully settled, it was time for school to begin. If we had still been in Alaska, little Sammy would have been in kindergarten, but Ironton didn't have public kindergarten so he stayed home one more year with Mother. Jason and I enrolled at the school two blocks down the street from the church. He was in the seventh grade, and I was in the fourth.

Jason and I were comfortable in the three story school in Fairbanks that housed all the kids from kindergarten through high school. Our new school in Ohio housed only kids from first through eighth grades. The school was new to us, but it wasn't a new building. It looked to me like it was at least a hundred years old. It was an old four story building that sat in the middle of a city block. A dirt playground surrounded the school, and I don't recall seeing a blade of grass anywhere on that block. A broad sidewalk led from the street through the middle of the dusty school yard, directly to the school's front door. You entered the building onto the second floor via a wide set of exterior stairs; this level was the location of the principal's office. Rickety fire escapes descended down each side of the large, frame, square schoolhouse.

In the 1940s Alaska's schools were very advanced so Jason and I were both academically ahead of the Ohio kids. Academics may have been easy in Ohio, but we were still unfamiliar with some of the traditions of our new school. In Alaska we were forced to attend school half days because of the extreme crowding. For this reason, and also because of the bitter Alaskan cold, neither of us had much experience with recess. Recess was a big deal in Ohio, and I loved it. On the back side of the Ohio school they had some playground equipment that fascinated me. I have never seen this same equipment on any other school ground anywhere. Because it was so unsafe, I'm confident it was outlawed long ago.

We called this popular playground contraption the "giant stride." It was a tall metal pole with long chains extending from its top. On the end of each chain was a two-step ladder, and twelve chains hung from the top of the pole. A dozen of us kids would each grab a chain, and then run as fast as we could in a circle several yards out from the pole. When we picked up enough speed, each of us jumped onto the ladder on the end of the chain. Centrifugal force then caused us to fly around and around the pole several feet above the ground. The giant stride was incredibly exhilarating, and we all jostled back and forth during recess for a turn on this dangerous toy. Kids often got hit by the swinging chains, or some fell off as we went flying around the pole. Almost daily someone was hurt playing on the giant stride, but we still couldn't wait for recess to get a turn.

Jason and I both did very well in our classes, but Jason had one experience in the Ohio school that he will never forget. Our principal was a stern, mean man; all the kids were afraid of him.

One day something happened in class, and the teacher sent Jason to the principal's office. It probably wasn't anything bad, but Jason was scared to death. Mother and Dad made it clear to us that if we got into trouble at school, we would face double jeopardy at home. Consequently, we never got into trouble. After the incident was all over, Jason said he didn't know what happened to him, but when the teacher sent him to the office, he didn't go.

Instead, he bolted out the front door of the school, down the steps, across the long sidewalk, and ran all the way home. When he got home, he didn't know what to do so he hid in his bedroom. Sooner or later, he knew he would have to face Mother and Dad, but I think he believed that he could wait until I came home for lunch. Then he thought that somehow he would get into the kitchen and make it back to school with me, and Mom and Dad would never know. It was just one of those situations that gets out of hand, and as an inexperienced adolescent, Jason simply didn't know how to handle it.

Before I ever got home for lunch, though, there was a knock at the door. When Mother went to the door, she was face to face with the truant officer. Our mean principal had sent him to our house to pick up one of his very best students—as though he were a criminal. When Mother and Dad realized what had happened, Jason wasn't in trouble at all. Dad went down to the school and had a good talk with the principal and the teacher. That never happened again—ever!

Our Ohio school had some customs unlike any in Alaska. In the fourth grade we were learning the multiplication tables; we drilled over and over on them until we knew them frontwards and backwards. Perhaps it was only my class, but whenever we finished an assignment, we shouted out: "I'm through." I got a big kick out of this because I was usually one of the first finished. Now, I know that this was not a good thing for the kids who worked slowly. But, when I was nine, it was fun.

The most curious thing they did in the Ironton schools in 1952, though, occurred on Monday mornings. The principal visited each class and asked for a show of hands of those who went to church, Sunday school, or mass the Sunday before. Whichever class had the highest percentage of church attendees received a large banner. Every week we anxiously awaited the Sunday school banner announcement, and it was a big honor to display the big blue felt Sunday School banner during the next week.

Before we left Fairbanks, I began piano lessens, and Mother wanted me to continue them once we were settled. Our church music director was hired as my piano teacher. We didn't own a piano so I had to practice next door in the church basement. One day when I finished practicing, I was headed up the concrete basement stairs to go outside and play. On the way up the stairs I tripped, hit my face on the right angle of the stairs, and broke my chin. What a mess I was. There was nothing the doctor could do but let my chin heal itself and hope for the best. Fortunately, I had no lasting negative results from that fall, but the temporary results were humiliating and embarrassing.

My face turned black and blue from ear to ear and remained that way for days. My teacher that year was young and pretty, and I thought she was wonderful. One day while my face was still black and blue, she asked me to take a note downstairs to another teacher. I thought it was so special that she asked me to run this errand, but my curiosity got the best of me. I took a peek at the note, and that was my big mistake. The note pointed out my black and blue face for my teacher's colleague to see. I couldn't believe that my wonderful teacher used me for such an errand. I was nearly in tears, but I never told her that I looked at the note. Even though she embarrassed me, it was hard for me to stay mad at her; in fact, I still remember her name—Miss Mayfield.

Mary Phyllis and I made our fourth grade class the most unique class in the building. I had just lived five years in the arctic and had traveled all over the western half of the United States. In February of 1950 our family traveled thousands of miles up the Alcan Highway through horrendous arctic conditions, and just that summer before fourth grade we traveled completely across the United States. Mary Phyllis was back home after five years in the jungles along the Amazon River of Peru. Both of us were full of stories of adventure and travel far beyond the Ohio River Valley. We brought treasures and pictures to the school that must have been mind boggling to the other kids. As much as we liked to talk about Alaska and Peru, Mary Phyllis and I still wanted most of all to fit in and be like the other kids.

During our brief visit in Upstate New York with Mother's new found relatives, my cousin taught me to ride a bicycle. Now, I wanted a bicycle of my own. When Christmas came, Jason and I were absorbed in holiday activities at the school and church. There were programs of all sorts and activities of many kinds. As exciting as all this was, a bicycle of my own was all I could think about. After badgering Mother and Dad repeatedly for a bicycle, they sat the three of us down. Kindly, they explained that because of the big summer trip, the new furniture, and the new car there wasn't enough money to buy large gifts of any kind that Christmas.

I had no idea what Dad's salary was, even though I knew it had to be more at this large church in Ohio than it was at the mission in Alaska. I also knew that we had been exceptionally fortunate to take such a big trip. As much as I could, I understood that this would be a "skimpy" Christmas. Jason and I both tried to buck up and be strong; we knew that Christmas was really about giving and being with family and celebrating Christ's birth. Dad and Mom were true to their word. Our Christmas tree was scrawny and nothing like the hand cut trees we had in Fairbanks. What looked most meager, though, was the lack of presents beneath the tree. There were pitifully few gifts.

Our tradition was to open gifts on Christmas Eve after Dad read the Christmas story from the Bible. By the looks of our pitiful tree, our 1952 gift opening promised to be exceedingly brief. Even when we dragged the ritual out and opened one gift at a time, it just wasn't going to take long to open the little dab of presents beneath our puny tree. After we opened our last gifts, Jason and I tried to sound appreciative and feel happy despite our disappointment. After all, we were kids who were accustomed to a lot more presents under the tree, as well as having dozens of friends near by. In Ohio we knew few people, and there were few gifts.

Mother and Dad baffled us, though, when they told us that there was one last gift for each of us, but we had to hunt for it. We had no idea what to look for or where to look. First, we went upstairs and looked in Mom and Dad's bedroom, in their closet, and under their bed. Nothing. Then, we checked our own rooms, thinking someone might have hid something there while we were at the Christmas Eve service. Again, nothing. We checked the dining room with its built-in hutch. It revealed nothing either. We looked on the back porch and on the large front porch. Everywhere we looked, we brought up a blank. But it didn't seem like Mother and Dad were kidding.

There was something else for each of us that Christmas, but we didn't have a clue what it could be or where it was. The only place left to look was the cellar-like basement of our old house. That cellar was so foreboding that we seldom ventured down there. Jason and I had the idea at the same time, and we nearly crashed as we headed down the steep cellar stairs. Of course, little Sammy was close on our heels. The only light in the basement was a single bulb that hung from the ceiling with a dirty little pull string. Jason grabbed the string, and there they stood.

Standing on the dirt floor in the middle of that musty basement stood two brand new shiny J.C. Higgins bicycles. Jason's was a brown "boy's" bike, and my "girl's" bike was blue. Each bike had a double headlight, white-walled balloon tires, a rear rider's seat, a horn, front and back reflectors, and a kickstand. They gleamed and they were gorgeous. Standing beside our bikes stood a miniature bicycle for Sammy—complete with training wheels. I don't know how my folks got the money for those bikes, but they certainly surprised Jason and me. We could hardly wait for Christmas Day so we could go outside and ride our very own splendid new bicycles.

Christmas – 1952

We had a blast on our bicycles. We rode them day after day and block after endless block. There seemed to be no end to what we could do or where we could go on our bikes. In the 1950s no one was fearful of strangers or talked much about harm and danger. Schools didn't teach classes on self-defense or give talks about a "Safe Place." In contrast to today, life was innocent, and strangers were friendly. It didn't seem to me that there was any danger other than the "Red

Menace" far away in Russia. As it turned out, I should have been more cautious than I was because the biggest and most potentially harmful scare of my childhood happened to me while I was riding my bike.

One afternoon in the spring, Jason and I were riding around the neighborhood with one of his friends. Since I was the little sister, they made me bring up the rear. I didn't care because being with them was fun; it was a big deal that they even let me go. Near the elementary school was the local high school with its football field and oval track. The three of us discovered a steep incline between the bleachers where we could shoot at a rapid pace straight down onto the track below. One after the other, we took off like crazy on our bikes straight down the incline and then sped swiftly around the track. It was daring, exhilarating, and dangerous. I'm sure Mother wouldn't have approved, but she didn't know.

Once one of us took off down the incline to the track below, we were completely out of reach until the next biker came roaring down the hill behind us. Jason and his friend took their turns first while I waited at the top of the incline. As I waited poised on my bike between the bleachers until it was safe for me to take off, a man jumped out of the bushes beside me. Before I hardly noticed him, he grabbed me in my most private place. I was shocked. No one had ever explained or even suggested such a scenario to me. As well as being stunned, I was instantly afraid. How dare he? I may have been only nine years old, but I knew this was wrong, and I was just as mad as I was afraid.

It all happened so fast; my mind was racing and my body was shaking from head to toe. I couldn't even imagine what he was thinking. As quick as a flash and without much thought, spontaneously my right hand flew out and slapped that man across the face as hard as any mad nine year old could slap. All the while, I kept my left hand on the handle bars to steady myself. I'm sure the slap wasn't very hard, but now he was the one who was stunned. In a reflex, he jerked his hand a way, and that's when I made my move.

I gave that bicycle all I had, and away I went flying down the hill. I was so frightened that not only was I shaking to beat the band, but the bike was quivering. It's a wonder that I made it to the bottom without taking a dreadful spill, but somehow I succeeded to make it in an upright position. When I caught up with Jason and his friend, I didn't tell them exactly what the man did, but I did convince them how afraid I was. They didn't think it was very serious and laughed at me for being a "scaredy cat" girl. But I knew that I had miraculously escaped great potential harm. It wasn't until I was much older that I realized how close I came that day to being the victim of sexual violence and/or abduction.

As soon as my shaking calmed down, I rode back to the safety of my home. Later that evening I described the event to my father. He listened attentively, but I don't think he fully understood how serious it was either. The incident was never reported, and it was never repeated. I'll never know who that man was or if he knew where I lived, but for days after that I was always looking over my shoulder to see if someone was following. All I know is that an angel was watching over me that day and that I kept a clear head and got myself out of a terrible predicament.

After that experience, the rest of my fourth grade year seemed rather mild. Each day we walked home from school at lunchtime. On the way back to school, we often stopped at a tiny little neighborhood store and bought some "Lickum Aid." Basically, "Lickum Aid" was slightly sweetened Kool-Aid in small packages that sold for a penny each. We poured the orange or grape or cherry "Lickum Aid" into our hand and licked it off and thought it was great. When we got back to school, we always had stained palms from this little treat. My fourth grade year was also the year that I learned to work a yo-yo. In Alaska I learned how to manipulate an Eskimo yo-yo, but it was much more important for me now to learn how to work a "real" yo-yo like the other kids.

Television was still new in 1953, and we certainly didn't own a set. The fact was that most people didn't own TVs then; my perception was that only the affluent had them. 1953 was the year of the coronation of Queen Elizabeth II. Behind the school was an annex—much smaller than the church annex, but still a building large enough to hold several classes at the same time. Someone brought a small black and white TV to school, and all us kids sat together in that small annex and watched the queen's coronation on a tiny little screen. The TV we watched was primitive compared to big screen TVs and lap top computers, but it was just as exciting to me as if I were in London in person. The queen had two small children (Charles and Ann) who were close in age to Jason and me. As I watched the coronation, I fantasized what life would be like to be a princess like little Princess Anne.

1952 and 1953 were big years; Dwight Eisenhower ran for president and the queen was crowned. When Eisenhower made a whistle stop in Ironton, school was dismissed for the momentous occasion. Dad took us to the train depot where we heard Eisenhower speak while he stood on the flag-draped rear of the train. We didn't need TV; we had the real McCoy in person right here in our own town—a candidate for president of the United States. Queens and presidents; how much better could it get?

The people in Ironton were wonderful to Mom and Dad and us kids. But the truth was that Ohio was a completely different world from what we had grown to love in Alaska. Jason and I didn't know it, but sometime during 1953, Dad contacted his denomination and asked if there was any way we could return to Alaska. Many years later, Dad still felt badly about leaving Ohio after such a short stay. Before I knew it, my father was assigned to "pioneer" a church in Juneau—Alaska's capital. In retrospect this was a huge decision for Mom and Dad. They were relinquishing a large church and moving back to a place that didn't even have a church, but we were going back to Alaska. Dad said that "Alaska was in his blood and he just couldn't get away from it."

Almost before we could turn around, our school year in Ohio came to an end. The last day of school was Memorial Day; the Ironton school had a unique tradition for school closure. All the children brought arm loads of fresh flowers to school on the last day. The teachers distributed report cards, and then we walked together to the cemetery and decorated the graves. That was that. With a traditional little ceremony and a walk to the cemetery, our year in Ohio was finished.

Early the following morning, Dad put Mother, Sammy, and me on a bus headed for Oklahoma. Mother's sister Fran was also coming from Oregon with my cousin, Valerie. We planned to meet in Oklahoma for a big family reunion; then, the three of us would spend the summer in Medford with Aunt Fran and Gramma. Dad and Mother disassembled my bicycle and shipped it to Oregon so I would have it to ride during the summer. Dad and Jason spent June and July in Ironton, and then they drove across the country on the old Lincoln Highway and met us in Oregon. Once our family reunited in Oregon, our stay in Ohio and our colossal trip to the East was history. We were headed back home to Alaska and another brand new start.

Chapter 8
The Summer of 1953

It all happened rather quickly; at least for me, it did. 1952 was full of changes, and just when we were getting settled and somewhat accustomed to the East, we were moving again. Even though our stay in Ohio was brief, all of us were glad to be returning to Alaska. Many years later, Dad admitted that it would have been better to wait a year or two longer before we left Ohio. But Mother and Dad couldn't wait it seemed, and as soon as my last day of fourth grade came and went, Mother and Sammy and I were gone from Ohio. It would be over fifty years before I returned to the Ironton area for my first visit back.

When I did return, I discovered the church that Dad pastored was still the same, although the parsonage had been torn down, and a large fellowship hall was added. The tabernacle was completely gone and replaced with private homes. A school stood on the same block where I attended fourth grade, but it wasn't the building Jason and I attended. The old school was razed shortly after we left, and the school building that stood there in the 1990s was now showing signs of aging. The dangerous giant strides were replaced with brightly colored modern playground equipment. It was as though the old building we attended had never been there, but it is still as alive in my mind today as it was so many years ago.

Late in May 1953 on the day after school was dismissed for the summer, Dad and Jason drove Mother, Sammy, and me to the Greyhound bus terminal. It was so early when we left that it was still dark outside. As we hugged Dad and Jason, the three of us were telling them "good bye" for nearly two months. Mother and Sammy and I were on our way to Oklahoma to meet Aunt Fran and my cousin Valerie to attend a big family reunion. Jason and Dad were staying in Ironton until the end of July. They planned to join us later that summer in Medford, Oregon at Gramma's house.

The bus was dark and dreary, but soon the light of day began to peek across the horizon, brightening our little world. We were unraveling our journey of 1952, but this year we were traveling south and west, rather than north and east. For two days and nights we traveled on that bus. Within minutes after we left Ironton, we crossed the Ohio River and entered Kentucky. This bus didn't get lost on a detour like Dad did the year earlier. We drove through Kentucky, Tennessee, Arkansas, and finally into Oklahoma without incident. Our first stop was Oklahoma City. I was born there, but Mother and Dad moved to Texas when I was an infant so it was exciting to visit my real "home town."

As the bus pulled into Oklahoma City, I was fascinated by the Oklahoma capitol building and grounds. Today, the capitol building has a beautiful dome, but it hadn't been added yet in 1953. The building itself was a rather austere looking structure situated in the middle of a large grassy area right in the middle of the city. What struck me as most fascinating wasn't the building; it was the oil wells and pumps on the capitol grounds. Up and down they pumped, silently giving notice to the world that beneath this old Oklahoma red dirt was black gold.

Mother had dozens of cousins in Oklahoma, and our first stop was with Cousin Verna in Oklahoma City where we stayed three days. Air-conditioning in 1953 wasn't the same as the refrigeration people use today. An "air-conditioner" was merely a water cooler that people set on their front porch or in a window. This contraption filtered the air with cooled water and literally blew cool air into the house. The bigger the cooler, the more cool air it produced, and the coolest place in the house was right in front of the air-conditioner. Compared to these days, air-conditioners were primitive in 1953, but they still indicated technological progress.

Cousin Verna had an air-conditioner in her front room; I was thrilled. In Alaska we didn't need air-conditioning, but in Ohio we sure did. Yet, we didn't have it, and few people we knew did. Somehow, people managed by using fans and screen doors and pretty much sweated it out. It was especially hot and humid in Ironton along the Ohio River, and that heat was miserable during the summer of 1952. Cousin Verna was older than Mother, but she had a son my age. For the entire time we visited Cousin Verna, her son and I sat in front of their cooler and played Monopoly. It was great! Forget about going outside. In front of the cooler was the place to be.

Our next stop was in Norman south of Oklahoma City at the home of Cousins Glen and Lois. They had a daughter one year younger than I, and I loved visiting her. It was more fun than I ever could have imagined being with all this family. One day, Cousins Merle and Drew brought their two daughters, and together we all went to the Oklahoma City Zoo. I hadn't been to a zoo since we left San Antonio in 1947, and I thought this was one of the best days ever. The high point of the day at the zoo was buying snow cones. I had never had a snow cone before, although I certainly sucked on a lot of icicles in Alaska. Once I ate one of those sticky, syrupy, sweet ice treats, I was hooked.

After a few days in the Oklahoma City area, we drove west with Cousin Verna to Elk City for our reunion with Aunt Fran and Cousin Valerie from Oregon. There were so many people to see; every day we went to a different home or farm and met more and more of Mother's Oklahoma relatives. Gramma still had two brothers in that area: Uncle John, the patriarch of the Music clan, lived in town. He and his wife, Sally, were highly respected in the community, and everyone in Elk City seemed to know them. They, too, had a big air-conditioner setting on their porch along side the porch swing. We stayed with them a couple nights; then headed to the country.

Mother's Uncle Tobe and her Aunt Sally not only lived in the country, they personified country. Their farm was an old dirt farm where they had lived since they homesteaded in the early 1900s. Aunt Sally wore plain cotton dresses with a traditional Oklahoma sun bonnet to protect her from the blasting sun. Uncle Tobe wore faded overalls, a floppy old straw hat, and had a ubiquitous chew of tobacco stuffed in his jowls. They were indeed colorful characters. Because the two Music brothers, Tobe and John, both had wives named Sally, the family differentiated between them by calling the "country Sally," Aunt Sally Tobe

Uncle Tobe's place was similar to Aunt Ruth's West Texas ranch but more country and more primitive. There was certainly no air-conditioning on that old farm—not one bit! Each morning we were awakened early by the cock-a-doodle-doo of the farm roosters. Valerie and I stood in total astonishment as we watched Aunt Sally Tobe walk out in the yard, grab a chicken, and wring its neck. I had never seen anything in all my life like that—even at Aunt Ruth's ranch. Aunt Sally Tobe swung that poor chicken around until its head popped off in her hand. We thought it was hilarious when she set the chicken down; for a few seconds before it fell, it ran around with its head off. This fresh chicken became dinner. In the mornings Aunt Sally Tobe gave us baskets and sent us to the hen house to fetch eggs for breakfast. What country feasts she prepared; there was always plenty of fried chicken, potato salad, fresh watermelon, and home made ice cream.

Decades after Uncle Tobe and Aunt Sally Tobe were dead and gone, major oil companies drilled on their land and struck natural gas. All their lives Uncle Tobe and Aunt Sally Tobe scratched out a meager existence from the old red Oklahoma clay. During the depression, their family of five was one of the poorest of the Oklahoma poor. By sheer grit and dogged determination they hung on to their little spread in Western Oklahoma and kept the land. It wasn't much, they thought, but at least it would make a small inheritance for their three children.

When the mineral rights were all rightfully divided, my Mother's "dirt poor" Oklahoma cousins were wealthy. Their parents' dirt farm paid off big, and each of them received a tidy sum. I seriously doubt that the natural gas money would have changed the way Uncle Tobe and Aunt Sally Tobe lived one iota. They were simple, honest country folks who did the best they could through difficult times. It is humorous, though, to know that in the end, their scrubby little farm was worth a bundle.

Whenever we visited Elk City, we went to see my grandfather, Dad's father. Dad's mother died the month I was born so I never knew her, but Granddad and his second wife, Jewel, still lived in Elk City. Granddad was a good looking man; unfortunately, his disposition didn't match his good looks. I never understood why, but he was sour and foreboding. I wasn't afraid of him, but he didn't do anything to endear himself to me either. His wife, though, was another story. I don't know where Granddad found her or how he got her to marry him, but her temperament definitely matched her name; we affectionately called her "Gramma Jewel."

Granddad and Gramma Jewel's house was humble to say the least. It was situated at the edge of town on a dirt street. The house was meager and small; there was a front porch that opened to an undersized living room and one bedroom. Behind that was a tiny hall with a bath on one side and a small kitchen behind it. In the tiny back yard was a well from which Gramma Jewel drew water daily. Beside the kitchen sink, Granddad still kept a bucket and ladle for drinking fresh well water. Even though the house was small and modest, Gramma Jewel kept it spotless and clean as a pin, and her yard was breathtaking. She made the most of what she had, and the entire yard was a collage of brightly blooming flowers.

There never was much to do at Granddad's, and my brothers and I always found it boring. Gramma Jewel always had a bright and cheery disposition that matched the flowers in the yard, and that helped. Granddad was different. He spent most of his day rocking back and forth on the front porch with a fly swatter in his hand, swatting at flies. As he sat there he chewed tobacco and waxed eloquent on the world's awful conditions. I can still see him sitting on the porch, rocking and spitting; the zing and ping of the tobacco juice as he hit one bull's eye after another in the nearby spittoon are indelibly etched in my memory.

Regardless of Granddad's disposition, my father and mother always showed him proper respect and taught us to do the same.

Our Oklahoma visit continued; a couple of times we even went swimming in Elk City's public swimming pool. It was too cold in Alaska to swim, and besides that Dad didn't think it was proper for young girls to swim in the same pool with boys and men anyway, so swimming in the public pool was a big treat. Of course, I didn't know how to swim, so I stayed close to the edge of the pool. It was still thrilling to be at the pool with all the other kids, though; especially on hot, stuffy Oklahoma days.

Soon it was time for us to head to Oregon with Aunt Fran and Valerie. On our trip to Oregon we weren't going to travel by bus like we did between Ohio and Oklahoma. Mother and Aunt Fran bought train tickets to California. I remembered how much I loved the train trips in Alaska, and I just knew that this trip would be even more fun because I was with Valerie. Early one morning, the five of us boarded the train in Elk City and headed west. It was too expensive to get a sleeper, so we rode coach all the way to Northern California.

It was pleasurable traveling west on the train. We passed through many cities of interest, including Amarillo, Texas. Jason and Sammy and I stayed nearby twice on Aunt Ruth's ranch, but this was the first time I had ever been through the city of Amarillo. Later in my adult life I lived with my husband in the Texas Panhandle, and this desolate looking area became my home; I couldn't even imagine that, though, at ten years of age. We continued into Colorado. The train crossed the entire state of Colorado, climbing laboriously through and over the Rocky Mountains. I had been in Colorado in 1947, but I was older now, and it was exciting to see Pikes Peak, Vail, and Aspen as we rattled on mile after mile.

We continued across the states of Utah and Nevada. In Nevada we crossed the Sierra Nevada Mountains, a route that I would travel many times in my adult life, but our 1953 train trip was my first experience with Donner Pass and the treacherous Sierra Nevadas. Valerie and I were charmed when we went through the burgeoning new gambling mecca of Reno, Nevada. Regardless, Mother and Aunt Fran thoroughly advised us against the evils of gambling.

At last we arrived in Sacramento—California's state capital. There was no train service between Sacramento and Medford, so we caught the bus just north of Sacramento for the final couple hundred miles through Northern California. After we crossed the Oregon border, the bus passed through Ashland—the west coast home of the famous Shakespeare Festival. Just a few more miles north of Ashland, we arrived in Medford. Only one year after our family drove from the West to the East across the United States, we now completed another coast-to-coast trek across the United States—east to west. What a trip! What a life!

The rest of the summer of 1953 simply flew by, and what a terrific time Valerie and I had together. Aunt Fran's house was small, but Valerie willingly shared her bedroom with me. We didn't sleep there often, however. Aunt Fran was a terrific gardener, and her back yard looked like a page from a garden magazine. It was totally bordered by a healthy, six foot hedge. Inside the hedge were well-groomed flower beds—specifically roses. Uncle Ed was a carpenter, and he built their entire house. The crowning point of their house and yard—to me at least—was a large patio right outside the kitchen door and in the middle of their beautiful backyard.

Aunt Fran and Uncle Ed had a canvas yard swing on the patio along with a picnic table and a barbeque. These were all extravagances that we didn't have in Alaska, and their backyard seemed like a fairy world. Since the yard was so sheltered and the temperature inside Aunt Fran's house was so hot at night, Valerie and I slept on the patio most of the time. At the back of the yard behind the hedge, Uncle Ed's workshop and garage stood by the alley. Valerie and I were both good and obedient girls, and for this reason, we got by with things that summer that no one ever even suspicioned.

Once little Sammy and all the adults in the house were asleep, many nights Valerie and I sneaked out into the alley where we got into a lot of mischief. Two or three houses down the alley from Valerie's house, there was a house that had a loaded cherry tree. Those poor people who owned that tree! Little by little Valerie and I stripped their tree of most of its cherries. We couldn't bring any of them home so we just giggled and laughed and ate our way up and down the alley. We would have been in a bushel of trouble if our mothers found out, but they didn't. We thought it was funny, but it really wasn't very nice—or safe—for us to be running up and down the alley in the middle of the night eating the neighbors' cherries.

Gramma lived exactly one block away from Aunt Fran; they even had the same street number on their houses. The very best nights of all for Valerie and me were the nights we spent at Gramma's. Her place wasn't much to look at, but boy did we have fun there. When Gramma moved to Oregon after her second husband died, she bought a three car garage that set on the back of a lot. Her hopes were to live there temporarily until her son was out of school and she could afford to build a house.

In the meantime, Uncle Ed fixed up the three car garage for Gramma and her son. Although the house Gramma dreamed about never got built, she was still happy in her three car garage. Her tiny house had two little bedrooms, a small bathroom, and one large living area and kitchen combination. Uncle Ed added a screened-in porch on one side. Outside the porch, Gramma had the biggest weeping willow tree I ever saw, and under it she also had a canvas porch swing.

Gramma's life had always been tough, but the toughness only made her more colorful and delightful to be around. She had such a positive attitude about everything; she was a joy. Everyone in Mother's family had brown hair and brown eyes except Mother. She must have taken after her German father because she was fair skinned, and after our 1952 visit to the New York relatives, I knew that I looked like him as well. Valerie had deep brown eyes and brown hair, but I was a blond. That summer Gramma began calling me her "Little Golden Girl," a nickname that I cherished.

Gramma had a huge trunk full of old family photos which Valerie and I rummaged through hour after hour. Each picture had an accompanying story, and night after night Gramma regaled us with tales of the Oklahoma land run and her family's journey from Kentucky in the early 1900s. She loved to tell us about the Dust Bowl, the Great Depression, and life in an extended, loving family. From the looks of the pictures of Gramma when she was a teenager and young adult, Valerie and I decided that she and her sisters must have been "flappers."

Wow! Our grandmother—a flapper. Flappers were the young girls of the early 1900s who had "bobbed" hair and wore beautiful clothes. They danced and partied and over all had a wild time. This image of Gramma was all so different from the Gramma we knew, but the pictures didn't lie. One of Gramma's teenage girl friends was in over half of the pictures; the girl's name was Pearl Higgonbotham. Valerie and I thought this was the funniest name we ever heard. For years after that summer and even to this day, we talk about Gramma's girlhood friend, Pearl Hinkybottle.

After Gramma moved to Oregon with my mother's kid brother, she had a variety of different jobs. She worked as a cook for the famous Bear Creek Orchards near Medford. When my uncle attended the University of Oregon, she actually went with him to Eugene and worked as the fraternity house cook and housekeeper. The college kids could never upset her with their college pranks; each time they tried to trick her, she got them back, and they loved it. In 1953 Gramma had another unique job. She worked as the private cook and housekeeper for a retired priest at the Sacred Heart Catholic Hospital. Gramma was a devout Methodist, yet she had much respect for the clergy—regardless of denomination. She loved her job at the hospital, and they all adored her.

Medford's Sacred Heart Hospital stood on top of a high knoll that had a winding road upwards to the hospital at the top. From anywhere in Medford, you could see that hospital. This hospital on the hill stood directly across the street from Aunt Fran's house. Most people drove up the road, but Valerie and I thought driving up the hill was too easy. Many days we hiked up and down that knoll. The climb was steep and replete with underbrush and thistles. Nevertheless, there was a plus side to this challenging climb; wild strawberries grew all over the knoll. When we weren't sneaking up and down the alley at night eating the neighbors' cherries, we were climbing the knoll in the day, eating wild strawberries. It's a wonder that we didn't get sick, but we didn't, and no one ever really knew what we were doing.

Uncle Ed was an avid fisherman, and because of all his fishing, he and Aunt Fran knew the back roads of Southern Oregon well. We took numerous picnics and outings that summer to rivers with exotic names like the Rogue and the Applegate. I didn't know how to swim, but it was still fun wading in these rushing rivers—always safely encapsulated in an inner tube.

Near Klamath Falls is the highway to spectacular Crater Lake. This was always one of Gramma's favorite places, and she insisted that we go there. Crater Lake was born nearly 7,000 years ago when Mt. Mazama erupted and virtually collapsed, forming this magnificent lake with depths that extend nearly 2,000 feet. Geologists confirm that this eruption was one of the largest in the last 10,000 years. Crater Lake celebrated its 100th birthday as a national park in 2002 and is one of America's oldest national parks. Gramma loved to tell scary stories, and she frightened me beyond words with tales of airplanes and cars that disappeared into Crater Lake's depths and have never yet been discovered.

Another interesting place near Medford is the historic town of Jacksonville, Oregon. It was near Jacksonville that Indians slaughtered many settlers during Oregon's pioneer days. Aunt Fran and Mother took us to the historic Jacksonville cemetery; there we wandered among tombstones with inscriptions indicating how entire families were slaughtered by the Indians. It was eerie, but it was captivating also to learn about the rough pioneer days of America's Northwest.

My favorite excursion that summer was a trip to the Oregon Coast. Between Medford and the Coast is a town called "Drain." Gramma had such a great sense of humor, and she got a big kick out of insisting that we take a restroom break in Drain. Gramma loved the coast and taught us how to snap and pop kelp like a bull whip. Uncle Bill snapped a real bull whip back on Aunt Ruth's Texas ranch so we knew what Gramma was talking about. Together we combed the beaches for exotic shells, sand dollars, and trinkets of all sorts.

I was mesmerized when Gramma told me that on one of her trips to the coast, she lost her watch. On her next trip a few weeks later, she found her own watch on the beach. What were the chances of that? With Gramma, though, nearly anything was believable.

When Valerie and I weren't sneaking down the alley eating the neighbors' cherries, climbing the hospital knoll and eating strawberries, picnicking by a Northwest river, or combing the Oregon beaches, we rode our bicycles all over the neighborhood. It was an enchanting and glorious summer that quickly came to an end. Before we knew it, Dad and Jason arrived in the Chevy from Ohio.

Like he did six years earlier on our move to Fairbanks, Dad held an Alaska service in the Medford church. Then, one lovely summer day after our last "good byes" were said and the car was packed, Dad headed the little Chevy North toward Seattle where we began our journey in it fifteen months earlier. We were off to Alaska once again. None of us knew what we were headed into or the many changes that would occur during the next three years; but as usual, they promised to be adventuresome.

Chapter 9
Back to Alaska

After only one brief year outside, once again we were headed north to Alaska. When we left Medford, Dad drove north toward Seattle on the exact same route that he drove in 1947—old Highway 99. In 1953, though, we weren't flying to Alaska from Seattle. Dad and Mother made reservations for another cruise—this time north from Vancouver, British Columbia to Juneau, Alaska.

After we left Medford, Dad drove through the now familiar Oregon cities on old Highway 99. When we crossed the Columbia River at Portland, our first stop was again in Kelso and Longview to visit mother's two aunts one more time. This route was becoming all too familiar to our traveling family. Including our 1949 Christmas trip, this was our fourth time on Highway 99 since 1947—traveling either north or south.

We always anticipated our stops in Longview and Kelso. Aunt Pearl and her husband, Uncle Sid, were both from Oklahoma like all the other relatives, but they had migrated to the Northwest many years earlier to be near Gramma's oldest brother, Theo. In August of 1953, their yard was just as beautiful as it had been the previous spring. Mother's other aunt lived on a farm outside Kelso just a few miles from Longview. They're farm was fun, but we still preferred Aunt Pearl's house the best.

Our last two stateside visits were soon over. The adventurous summer of 1953 was nearing an end as we headed north toward Seattle and the Washington city of Port Angeles. Juneau has a much milder climate than Fairbanks, so it wasn't necessary for us to stop in Seattle and shop for winter clothes like we did in 1947. Following Dad's brief visit with two of his Seattle minister friends, we headed north again into brand new territory.

As was now their custom, Mom and Dad wanted us to benefit from these long journeys. Consequently, before we boarded the boat in Vancouver, they took one last side trip. We drove along the western shores of the Hood Canal in Washington State's beautiful Olympic Peninsula to the town of Port Angeles; there we boarded a ferry and crossed the Strait of Juan de Fuca to Victoria, B.C. Victoria is the capital of British Columbia, and it is one of the world's most charming cities. Mother and Dad took us to the provincial capitol building with all its Old World charm. In addition, we visited the world famous Empress Hotel. Although Dad didn't have enough money for us to enjoy their famous "High Tea," it was still fun to walk through the hotel lobby and gaze.

The most fascinating part of Victoria, though, is its breathtaking Butchart Gardens. This garden is the quintessential example of the frog that turned into a prince. At one time it was an abandoned rock quarry—an eye sore to the entire area. Jennie Butchart, the wife of the quarry owner, saw potential in this eye sore, and the rest is history. Today, Butchart Gardens is one of the most visited tourist attractions in the world. Strolling through the garden is like visiting Eden. Intertwined between its winding paths and walkways are begonia and rose gardens, ponds, and flora and fauna of all kinds. It is absolutely ethereal, and I felt like I was in heaven.

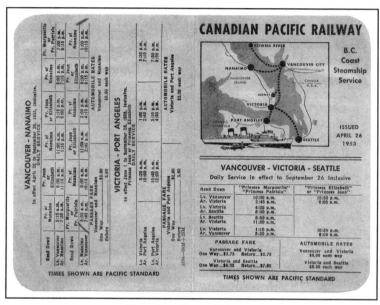

Nanaimo Ferry Schedule

Our stay in Victoria was brief, but memorable. Rather than return directly across the sound to Vancouver, Dad and Mom opted to drive up the coast of Vancouver Island to the port city of Nanaimo. This drive was spectacular as we drove along the coast of the island on the Georgia Strait. Across the narrow waters we could see little resorts and settlements on the main land. In just a few days we would be passing this way again on the steamship, but for now it was delightful to experience it by land. Following this brief two day side excursion, Dad drove the Chevy onto another ferry in Nanaimo, and we headed back east toward Vancouver and the steamship pier. In the spring of 1952 when we disembarked in Seattle from *the Baranof,* none of us had the slightest idea that in just a little over a year we would once again be boarding a steamship. What a lucky little girl I was!

Only one day remained before the steamship sailed to Alaska, so Mom and Dad took advantage of this day for sightseeing one last

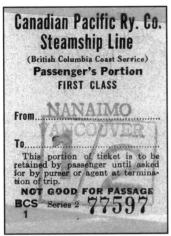

Ferry Ticket

time. Vancouver was initially a town called Granville that sprang up both because of its excellent warm water port and also because of the forestry that was so prevalent in the Pacific Northwest. When the trans-Canadian railroad crossed Canada, it chose Granville as its western terminus. The railroad didn't consider Granville a glamorous enough name for such a future city, so they changed its name to Vancouver. This name was rightfully chosen; the city was named after English Captain George Vancouver who first sailed these waters in 1792 on his ship, *the Discovery.*

Vancouver is Canada's third largest city and a world class city in its own right. Situated between Burrard Inlet and English Bay, it is breathtakingly beautiful. Like New York, London, and San Francisco, Vancouver has its own inner city garden—Stanley Park. Nestled in the middle of this modern city on prime real estate, stands this 1,000 acre park. What a park it is; within its perimeters you can find anything you want for relaxation: restaurants, a zoo, an outdoor theatre, a children's train, horse drawn carriages, and one of the world's most renown totem pole displays. The park is encircled by a sea walk, road, and bicycle path. On our one day in Vancouver, we visited Stanley Park and were as enchanted as we had been in Victoria's Butchart Gardens a few days earlier.

At the northern tip of Stanley Park where Burrard Inlet opens into the Georgia Strait, the waters are spanned by the beautiful Lion's Gate Bridge. In 1938, the wealthy Guinness family spent nearly six million dollars of their own funds to build a suspension bridge across the water in order to gain access to their land. This area opposite Stanley Park is now the modern setting of North and West Vancouver. In 1955 a new bridge was suggested to replace the dated Lion's Gate, but public sentiment was against it, and Lion's Gate was modernized and widened instead. In 1953 the Lion's Gate Bridge was Canada's gateway to the Inside Passage, and it still is today.

PURCHASER'S RECEIPT FOR FOREIGN DRAFT
THE FIRST NATIONAL BANK OF PORTLAND   No. 43007

MEDFORD   BRANCH   DATE   AUGUST 4, 1953

DRAWN ON   FOREIGN AMOUNT 288.89 $ 292.50

BANK OF NOVA SCOTIA, VANCOUVER   IN FAVOR OF MR. H.C. 'JAMES c/o CANADIAN PACIFIC RAIL-
                                                      WAY COMPANY
PURCHASER J. MELTON THOMAS

The First National Bank of Portland does not accept liability for any drafts which are not presented for payment promptly.   [Not Negotiable]
Refund, if necessary, will be made at the rate of exchange current at the time of such refund.   [Do Not Send Abroad]
                    THIS STUB TO BE DETACHED AND RETAINED BY PURCHASER

The check for our 1953 cruise

Shortly, it was time to board our ship at the Ballantyne Pier. In 1953 the Ballantyne Pier was the most prominent pier on Vancouver's waterfront, and although the 1982 Vancouver World's Fair gave the city the beautiful white-sailed Vancouver Place, the Ballantyne Pier is still used today. Dad and Mother bought passage to Juneau aboard *the Princess Louise,* a little steamship that belonged to the Canadian Pacific Railroad/Steamship Company. It was a beautiful ship, but none of us thought it was as magnificent as *the Baranof.* Perhaps our journey one year earlier had been so romantic and so adventuresome that it was difficult to top; nevertheless, we were thrilled to be aboard a steamship once again.

Since we were only sailing as far north as Juneau, this cruise wouldn't be as long as the 1952 cruise on *the Baranof*—or as expensive; our 1953 trip only cost $292.50 for the five of us. As I boarded the ship in August 1953, I remembered the early May morning just one year earlier when Mother and Dad and I slipped off *the Baranof* in the semi-darkness and walked the streets of Juneau. In 1952, I thought that would be my only visit to Juneau ever. Now, just one year later, Juneau was to be my new home. Many years after 1953, I was to visit Juneau weekly each summer when I lectured for the cruise lines, but I didn't know anything about that in 1953 as I boarded the *Princess Louise.* In August 1953, I was just a wide-eyed ten-year-old girl.

Our steamship tickets came in this attractive jacket

The Princess Louise was one of several Canadian Pacific "princess" ships, and was one of Canada's finest steamships that plied the Northwest waters. Twenty-five years later, I discovered *the Princess Louise* in the Long Beach, California harbor where it stood anchored, functioning then as a restaurant. Just a few years after I rediscovered my little ship in Long Beach, it burned and it is no more (*The Baranof* sank in the Mediterranean Sea. Both of my ships are gone.)

On a foggy morning after the little Chevy was lowered into the hold of the ship—August 19, 1953—we slipped away from Vancouver's Ballantyne Pier, sailed under the Lion's Gate Bridge, and headed north into the beautiful Canadian sector of the Inside Passage. In 1952 *the Baranof* sailed on the western side of Vancouver Island, down the Strait of Juan de

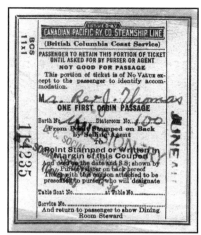

Dad's steamship ticket

Fuca, into Puget Sound, and docked in Seattle. In 1952, the *Princess Louise* sailed from Ballantyne Pier, past Prospect Point, and along the eastern side of the island via the Georgia Strait. Our staterooms were small and crowded, but the journey and the service were both fantastic. This was new territory for all of us, and it was scenic and breathtaking.

Because of his inclination to motion sickness, Jason dreaded the trip. The waters of the Inside Passage are narrow and sheltered; this keeps ships from being trapped in open, rough seas. In 1953 Jason fared much better than he did in 1952. The only waters where he could have had difficulty were the treacherous Seymour Narrows near the future site of the 2.2 million acre Great Bear Rainforest (See Appendix No. 5) or the Dixon Entrance just south of Ketchikan. Mother Nature was kind to us, and we sailed through the narrow straights on smooth seas.

The Princess Louise docked twice during our short cruise. We spent a half day in Prince Rupert, British Columbia, and then we stopped briefly in Ketchikan just across the border in United States territory. A hotel in Prince Rupert had a traveling display of an Egyptian mummy. I couldn't believe it; mummies were something brand new and totally different than anything I had ever seen. I stood in disbelief and awe looking at the remains of a man who had lived thousands of years earlier in a far distant land. He was wrapped in linen and was so well-composed that his features were distinguishable. I decided that the Egyptians must have been pretty intelligent people.

In 1952 I spent my own money to buy a souvenir at Valley Forge; now, I wanted a Canadian souvenir as well, and I wanted to purchase it with my own money. In a Prince Rupert gift shop, I found a bone china cream and sugar set with Queen Elizabeth's coronation photo on it. Earlier that year I remembered watching her coronation on the little black and white TV in the annex of my Ohio school. It cost every last penny that I had, but it was a real treasure that I have kept to this very day.

Almost as quickly as it began, our brief cruise on *the Princess Louise* came to an end. The captain maneuvered the little ship from the Chatham Strait into Stephens Passage, and finally into the narrow Gastineau Channel between Juneau on the mainland and Douglas Island across the channel. This was the reverse route that the captain of *the Baranof* took in 1952. Nothing has changed in this regard in fifty years; ships still sail in and out of Juneau the exact same way we did in 1952 and 1953. Just like that; *the Princess Louise* was at the Juneau dock. Our long journey across the United States and back was over. We were in our new home.

As we sailed up the Gastineau Channel, we passed the little settlement of Thane—the company town of the Juneau/Douglas Gold Mining Company. Just a little way farther up the channel, we passed Dupont Wharf where dynamite was off-loaded for the mines. The dynamite was kept at a distance from town for safety purposes, and it was brought to the mine in increments as needed. We docked facing the Juneau/Douglas mine that crawled from the tidewater straight up Mount Roberts. Modern day cruisers often don't even know what they are seeing when they ascend Mt. Roberts on the Mount Robert Tramway, but in 1953 the mine's superstructure covered the entire side of the mountain. This superstructure burned in the 1950s, and today there is little remaining evidence of this previously active and productive mine. Each year the underbrush covers more and more of the visible mine shafts, until eventually nothing of the mine will be visible at all.

Our 1953 arrival in Juneau was a great deal different than our arrival in Fairbanks in 1947. The mission in Fairbanks was weak when we arrived, but it was established and had been running rather well for over fifteen years. This was not the situation in Juneau. Dad was moving to Juneau to pioneer a brand new mission, and *nothing* was there. Since there was no mission, there were no people; consequently, there was a very small welcoming committee—one woman in fact!

Welcome back telegram from Fairbanks friends

Not only was there no building or no congregation, there was no where for our family to live; this presented a major concern for our family. We were warmly welcomed, though, by our Fairbanks friends.

We disembarked that August day in 1953 with little. The few meager personal items that Mother shipped ahead were waiting for us at the dock, including the blue trunk that by this time had traveled as much as we had. There was a barrel of dishes and other household necessities. Other than those items and the Chevy, we disembarked in Juneau with only the clothes on our backs. Dad had a dream of a thriving mission in this territorial capital, and he was eager to get started "digging it out" as he called it.

A place to live was our first and biggest concern. Dad's new mission was definitely on a budget, and the high housing costs far superseded the mission's meager budget. Our Juneau welcoming committee—the single lady who met us at the boat—owned and operated a boarding house. She invited us to live with her *and* her other boarders until Dad could get a feel for Juneau and find adequate housing for the family. That was our best offer, and although Dad and Mom were reluctant, they accepted her gracious invitation. So began one of the most interesting years of my life—life in a boarding house!

Chapter 10
The Boarding House

Living in a boarding house is one of the most challenging experiences any family can endure. Single families are meant to be together, to share their lives with one and other, and to work it out day by day. Sharing a part of your childhood with four complete strangers is a test for any family, and it certainly was for ours.

The lady who met us at the Juneau dock and the owner of the boarding house was one of the most distinctive individuals I have ever known. She was originally from Seattle, and like many other civilians, she made the trek to Alaska during the war to work for the government; she fell in love with Alaska and stayed. When we arrived in 1953, she worked for the Territory of Alaska and had lived in Juneau for several years. She was single, and somewhere along the line had been able to afford this most unique house.

Juneau's topography is one of the most distinctive in the world. It literally erupts from the sea and creeps precariously up Mt. Roberts. Over the years, Juneau's waterfront has been filled with tailings from the many mines so that there is some level land along the water, but not much of that had happened yet in 1953. Now, there are beautiful homes a few miles out of the city in "the valley" near world famous Mendenhall Glacier. In 1953, though, there were just a few dairy farms and homesteads near the glacier. In 1953 over ninety percent of Juneau's residents lived right on the side of the mountain or along the waterfront.

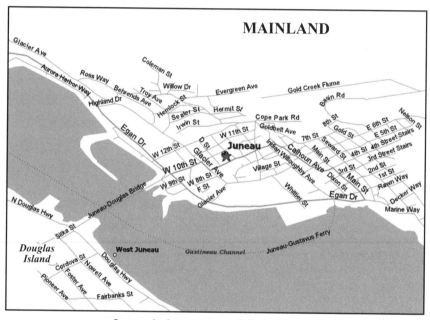

Juneau's downtown and dockside area

Juneau's streets are numbered as they ascend the mountain from Franklin Street near the waterfront, and they climb consecutively up the steep incline of Mt. Roberts. The numbered streets are perpendicular with the waterfront, and each numbered street intersects streets such as Main, Seward, or Gold. Franklin Street is Juneau's main artery, and after it passes through the downtown area, it becomes Egan Drive. This is the road that leads to the valley and Mendenhall Glacier. Because the numbered streets literally ascend the mountain, it is not uncommon in the winter especially when roads are slick to see a car from Sixth or Seventh Street rush pell-mell down the mountainside toward the water—or even land in the water for that matter.

Our new home—the boarding house—was on Seventh Street. I've never seen anything completely like it, even to this day. Because the house was built on the side of the mountain, it looked different from each direction. It was actually a two story house with a high pitched attic. If you looked at it as you climbed the mountain, though, it looked like a four story house. From Seventh Street, it was only a two story house that was built right along the sidewalk with one level beneath the ground.

The large house had many rooms. Entering the front door, you walked through a small vestibule built to keep cold winds outside. From this small vestibule, you stepped directly into a good sized living room that had a fireplace with a mantel. The main level had three bedrooms and one bath on the street side of the house. The living room joined to a medium sized dining room that had a swinging door opening into a small kitchen. This was really a grand old house, and it appeared as though the kitchen was intended only for cooking. Eventually, Mother and Dad set up a tiny breakfast table in the kitchen, but all our evening meals were eaten in the larger dining room.

The kitchen had two doorways back to back; one led up a steep stairway to the second floor; the other led to the basement. From the second floor, there was yet another stairway leading to a third floor attic. The second floor had a bedroom on either side of a narrow hall and one small room at the end of the hall. The second flight of stairs from the kitchen led down to a damp, dark, and dismal basement. The basement held the furnace and a typical collection of junk.

It was unusual in Juneau even to have a backyard if your house sat on the mountain, and yet this house had a pretty good sized backyard. It was rather unkempt and very steep since it was on the incline side of the house. The backyard was fenced and had some overgrown raspberry bushes that I found inviting. In addition to the front door, the only other exit door to the entire house was from the basement into the backyard.

Because the house had only two exits, its crowning feature was a metal fire escape. That's right. Because she took in boarders, and since the house had so many levels and only two exits, the city required the owner to provide an additional escape. The fire escape reminded me of pictures I had seen in the *Saturday Evening Post* of tenement houses in America's large cities. It was a folding metal contraption that could be unfolded downward if ever necessary. When someone stepped on it, that person's weight forced the metal escape to unfold until it finally met the ground. It was reminiscent of our school fire escape in Ironton. It seemed funny to me to be living in a house with a fire escape, but that's the way it was.

The boarding house seemed gigantic, but there were a lot of people living in it. When our family arrived in 1953, the owner already had two other single women living there. Our family of five more made eight boarders in the big old house. It was an arrangement that can't be compared to anything else. There was only one bathroom—the one on the main floor, and Dad and Jason were the only men in the house. Each of the ladies worked for the territory, and soon my mother was working there as well. To say the least, getting ready for school or work in the morning was a challenge for everyone.

One of the main floor bedrooms was already rented; and the owner willingly vacated her room beside the bath and gave it to my parents. Sammy and I shared the other main floor bedroom. The owner then moved to the second floor across the hall from her other renter, while Jason took the bedroom at the end of the hall. No one was on the very top level, and that's a good thing because I don't think that house could have handled anyone else. Mother accepted responsibility for the cooking, and our family pretty much took over the entire house. For the time being at least, this would be "our" home. Regardless, all eight of us would share evening meals together around the large dining room table.

The lady who owned the boarding house was as unusual as the house itself. She was a modest and wholesome woman, but she was the shiest adult I've ever known; she blushed if you looked at her sideways. Because she was so shy, she didn't say much to anyone, and when someone spoke to her, she just giggled. It was the oddest thing I'd ever seen. She had a habit that intrigued me; she bit her fingernails—constantly. I was fascinated. She bit them into the quick. Perhaps it was her shyness, but she never stopped biting her nails. Living with a family—especially with three growing kids—was indeed a sacrifice to her; and it's really no wonder that she bit her nails. We probably drove her to it. She sincerely wanted a church in Juneau, though, and I believe that offering us a place to live was her way of helping out. She has long since passed away, and I'm certain there must be a special reward for this dear woman for putting up with us.

Although she was different and shy, the boarding house owner was nice and tried her best to get along with everyone. I think in her own shy way she enjoyed the excitement and activity that our family brought to her big old house. Her second floor renter was nice also and never caused us any grief. The lady who lived downstairs in the bedroom next to Sammy and me, though, was a different story. She was a fussy old widow who thought she knew everything about raising kids.

In 1953, Jason was beginning adolescence, and Mother and Dad weren't sure how to handle him half the time themselves. They definitely didn't need help from this old lady. Within a few months of our arrival at the boarding house, she moved out, and we were all glad. I'm not sure if we chased her away or if she moved out of town, but we most definitely didn't go looking for her. After she moved out, it was just the seven of us, and things went as well as could be expected under such irregular circumstances.

Dad took a sacrificial pay cut to move back to Alaska and start this new mission. After five years in Fairbanks, the church was paying him a good salary, and the church in Ohio paid him well also. That was not the case in Juneau. Dad received a very small monthly stipend from his general church headquarters; this was most assuredly not enough to support our family even with the "good deal" of living in the boarding house.

Mother's job at Pan American during our last year in Fairbanks was a great job for her in more ways than one. Her salary afforded our family many luxuries over the next couple of years: We were able to take the cruise outside on *the Baranof;* Mom and Dad bought the new Chevy; and they were able to purchase an entire house full of furniture for the parsonage in Ironton. But the biggest perk of all from Mother's job at Pan Am was that it introduced her into the work place. As it turned out, Mother was an excellent bookkeeper.

Within days after our arrival in Juneau, Mother took the Civil Service test. No one was surprised when she passed with flying colors and was offered another excellent job—this time working for the Territory of Alaska. Juneau was the territorial capital so all of the various departments were located right there in town. Within a month after our arrival in Juneau, then, Mother went to work in a lovely, modern office building just four blocks down the hill from the boarding house. This was the same building that Mother and Dad and I had walked past in the pre-dawn stillness in May of 1952. Who would have thought?

Two blocks down the hill from the boarding house (or up the hill depending on the direction you were going) was Juneau's Elementary School. It faced Fifth Street and sat directly across the street from the high school. That was it for Juneau schools in 1953: one elementary school for kindergarten through eighth grades and one high school next door. Across the channel on Douglas Island, there was an elementary school, but the high schoolers crossed the bridge each day to Juneau High. Since our arrival was in late August, it was immediately time to enroll in school.

1953 was my fifth grade year; it was Jason's eighth grade, and finally, Sammy began first grade. For the only time in our lives, all three of us attended school in the same building. The school was about a five minute walk from the boarding house, and it was easy to get there—just run down the hill. Climbing back up the hill to the boarding house took forever. The only kids who ate lunch at school were the kids who lived out in the valley near the glacier, so each day all three of us walked home for lunch—up the hill!

Similar to our school in Ironton, the Juneau school had three stories with a playground surrounding it. Unlike our school in Ohio, there were no playground toys. It rains too much in Juneau for that. The main entrance with its large double doors was on Fifth Street. Because the school building had to adapt to the incline of the mountain, it had an unusual feature. Since Juneau's streets were so steep, a footbridge stretched from the third floor across the playground and onto Sixth Street. It was fun to go to the third floor of the school, walk across a bridge three stories above ground and come out onto a completely different street—all the while looking at kids playing on the playground two stories below. That was Juneau, and people were accustomed to unusual buildings. It wasn't uncommon, for instance, for someone to have fifty or sixty stairs from the street up to their home. Even today, some of these stairs have names just like streets.

All three of us loved our teachers and our new school. My teacher our first year in Juneau was Miss Hermes. I LOVED her, and it was she who inspired me to eventually become an educator. In 2003—fifty years after my fifth grade year—I visited her at her home on Douglas Island. I was surprised to discover that she remembered me as much as I remembered our year together so many years earlier.

Mother was hired to work for the Territorial Welfare Department in "Aid to Dependent Children." The territorial office building sat catty-cornered from the capitol building on one corner and the city library on the other. It was a four story office building with a main entrance and lobby in the middle of the first floor. Mother's office was to the left at the end of the first floor hall. Six women worked in her office—an office that had the most unusual characteristic I've ever seen. Each of the six desks faced a glassed in office where their boss worked; all day, everyday, he was watching them. It was weird.

Alaska is huge, and Mother wrote welfare checks for the territory to some villages thousands of miles away. Many of the welfare recipients were Native Americans, and Mother quickly came to understand some of their culture. Alaska's clans are predominantly matriarchal; a child's first name would be his mother's last name, and each child's last name would be something totally different. In addition to this oddity, many Natives were enamored with American history tidbits. Often their children's last names would be Washington or Jefferson or Lincoln. It was difficult to track recipients in the same family with this unusual system, and what stories Mother had to tell each evening during dinner Despite the fact that she was being "watched," Mother loved her new job, and our family was thankful for it. In a word, we would not have survived in Juneau if Mother had not gotten such a good job.

For the five years we lived in Fairbanks and the three years we lived in Juneau, I don't remember once that we went out to a restaurant to eat. Eating out just wasn't part of our lifestyle during those financially tight years. This meant that living in a boarding house and working full time, Mother was taxed to the limit when it came to household responsibilities. Mother was a good cook, and our family was glad for this because we had no idea how or even "if" the three boarding house ladies knew how to cook. Even though Mother promised to do the cooking and shopping, before the year was over, Jason and I were doing a great deal of the cooking for all eight of us.

Before we left Fairbanks, I began taking piano lessons, and I continued them in Ironton—even to the tune of a broken chin. Against the dining room wall of the boarding house stood an old upright piano. We were all thrilled because this meant that Jason and I could continue our lessons. As soon as she could after we got settled in Juneau, Mother found us a good piano teacher. Once school began, I fell into a rather adult routine. Mother and Dad insisted that I get as much of my school work done as possible during the school day. When I got home from school I practiced the piano one whole hour. This wasn't particularly easy since Jason was taking piano lessons also, and he was supposed to practice an hour as well. Between the two of us, we took turns supervising little Sammy while the other one practiced. Or, at least that was the way it was supposed to be in theory.

Mother came home from her office for lunch every day, and Dad met us unless he was involved in something for the mission. After we lunched on something quick and easy, Mother began supper preparations. Very quickly, it was evident that she needed help, and I was the appointed helper. Before I returned to school after lunch, she set out exactly what we were to have for dinner that night—for our family and for the three ladies. To begin with she only expected me to complete some minor jobs to help with dinner preparations. Soon she learned that I was good at it. Little by little the responsibility of supper was handed over to me. I can't say that I cooked dinner alone each night, but I sure did a large portion of it. I actually learned how to cook while we lived at the boarding house.

I learned to cook at the boarding house, but I fell in love with baking. Very soon I was better at making pies than Mother. 1953 and 1954 were the years when *Betty Crocker* and *Duncan Hines* changed cake baking forever when they "invented" cake mixes. I took to cake mixes like crazy. Before cake mixes, all baking was done "from scratch," so these new-fangled mixes were all the rage and a sure sign of progress. It was easy for a young girl like me to get pretty good at making cakes when all I had to do was stir in water and eggs, put the layers in the oven, and bake.

1953 was years before the introduction of *Teflon*. Baking cakes was easy, but getting cake layers out of the pans without the cake sticking was difficult, so Mother taught me how to "flour" the pans: First, she rubbed the bottom of the cake pans with *Crisco* and then sprinkled flour on top of the *Crisco*. Next, she shook the flour around until it adhered to the *Crisco*. The trick to getting cake layers to come out of the pan easily was to make sure flour covered every spot of the bottom and sides of the pan. Then, when the cake was finished, all I had to do was turn the pan upside down on a cooling rack, and "wahla," I had a perfect cake layer. Good cakes demanded icing so I experimented with powdered sugar and milk or water mixed with dark chocolate until I got pretty good at making cake icing, too.

One day I thought my fellow boarding house residents would enjoy a treat. In one of Mother's cookbooks I found a picture and directions for making a jelly roll. Mother had never made a jelly roll, but I thought that surely I could follow the directions and come up with something as pretty as the picture in the book. "How difficult could it be?" I thought. I followed all the directions, but I couldn't get the thin cake to roll without breaking. What a mess I made. It looked like a folded, broken pancake with a little jelly in it and some powdered sugar on top. I was embarrassed with the result and never tried that again.

Because of the fun I was having in the kitchen, I learned more and more. Before the end of my fifth grade year, I knew how to fry chicken, how to peal and boil potatoes and then mash them with Mother's hand masher, how to prepare vegetables for stew, how to cook pudding on the stove top, how to make *Jell-O* salad—and green salad when we could afford the greens. Mother said that the best way to learn is by doing, and she sure needed help; so I tried. Often, I made a mess, but everyone was tolerant with my cooking attempts. Mother still made the things she thought were too difficult for me, but I learned a lot about cooking that year, and it has stood me in good stead ever since.

One dish I learned to cook during our year at the boarding house is a delicacy today. It's called "halibut cheeks," and today it's a costly dish in fine restaurants. But during our days in the boarding house, the ladies and our family ate halibut cheeks "for free." Halibut cheeks are tender pieces of meat cut from beneath a halibut's eye;

restaurants coat them in tempura batter and deep fry them. In the '50s few people outside of Alaska had discovered halibut cheeks yet, but Mother knew about them. Sometimes, she sent Jason to the docks, and if he was lucky, he got a fisherman to give him the halibut cheeks before he tossed the head into the sea. It was as simple as that. Mother didn't fry the halibut cheeks in tempura batter; rather, she rolled them in milk, coated them in corn meal, and then fried them. Soon, I was frying halibut cheeks as well as Mother. They were delicious and high on the menu wish list with all the boarders.

Eventually, our family fell into the unusual routine of sharing our lives with three single women. For the most part, we all made the best of it, but sometimes it was complicated. We seldom had any privacy; consequently, anything and everything that went on in the family was public knowledge in our little boarding house world. I know that Mother and Dad were doing the best they could, but board-ing house life is not a life that I would ever recommend for quality family life.

Chapter 11
Historic Juneau

Volumes have been written about the Klondike Gold Rush of 1898 and 1899. The epic story of the steamships *Portland* and *Excelsior* docking in Seattle and San Francisco loaded with thousands of dollars in gold and dozens of newborn millionaires is now legendary. With the arrivals of these two steamships, the world was on the move to Alaska and the Canadian Klondike. The adage "timing is everything" certainly was true for the Klondike Gold Rush. At that specific time, the United States was experiencing a depression, and even the suggestion of sudden riches was too much for hundreds of hungry men and a few brave women to withstand.

Newspapers around the globe heralded the arrivals in Seattle and San Francisco of these two little steamers from the far north. Within days after the arrivals of *the Excelsior* and *the Portland*, the "rush" was on to the North. The world had never seen anything like it then, and it hasn't since. Because of the depression of 1899, this was predominantly a white collar rush. Bankers, brokers, city officials, law enforcement officers, senators, clergymen, school teachers, and businessmen alike were all infected with "Klondicitus."

The 1899 Klondike Gold Rush, however, was not Alaska's first big rush. Since the days of the Russians, there had been rumors of gold and copper and other untapped natural resources in this frozen northern wilderness. These rumors beckoned a unique breed of men and women to the North. Alaska's early settlers weren't white collar workers struggling to get rich in a hurry; not at all. These men and women were rough, seasoned, and determined "sourdoughs." For example, George Carmack and Skookum Jim, the co-discoverers of Klondike gold and the ones responsible for beginning the stampede of 1899, had been in Alaska for years when they hit pay dirt and struck it rich.

Twenty years before the world ever heard about the Klondike, gold was discovered at the site of present day Juneau. In 1880 a speculator named George Pilz from Sitka sent Richard Harris and Joe Juneau to the area to grubstake for him. Rumors were rampant about possible gold in this area, and Pilz wanted to be a part of the strike when it happened. Joe Juneau was an illiterate French Canadian who spent more time drinking than he did prospecting, while Richard Harris was more the brains of the twosome. On their initial trip to the area, these two men were discouraged by the severity of the region near Mt. Juneau and Mt. Roberts, and they quickly lost interest in the search, returning to Sitka empty handed.

Pilz was undeterred by their indifferent attitudes and actions and sent Harris and Juneau back on a second gold seeking mission. This time they consulted Tglingit Chief Kowee and promised him one hundred *Hudson's Bay* blankets if he would take them to the rumored sites of gold. Chief Kowee led them from the mouth of the creek up a gulch and into a basin where they found some "color" in the stream. In addition, they discovered gold embedded in quartz. Miners referred to this embedded gold as *gold flour*.

Most assuredly, this was Pilz' anticipated Mother Lode, and it turned out to be one of the most lucrative and productive sources of gold in all Alaska. Harris and Juneau appropriately named the rushing creek that tumbled and swirled down the back side of Mt Roberts, "Gold Creek." And the rush for gold was on to the Juneau area. Unlike the Klondike strike twenty years later, news of this strike didn't circulate in the lower forty-eight. The prospectors who rushed to Juneau lived nearby in villages and on islands. In contrast to the Klondike, it didn't take miners a year to reach the strike site, and they didn't need a thousand pounds of supplies to survive. They were there almost overnight.

During the 1880s the famous naturalist, John Muir, and his missionary companion, Samuel Hall Young, extensively explored the glaciers, mountains, and islands of Southeast Alaska. Muir initially traveled to Alaska to confirm his theory that California's Yosemite Valley was glacially sculpted. Alaska became a working laboratory that not only proved his Yosemite theory, but at the same time, the land won his heart. When Harris and Juneau were returning to Sitka with news of the gold discovery, they accidentally encountered Muir and Young who had been exploring the Tracy Arm and nearby Sum-Dum Glacier just south of the area.

Harris knew that John Muir suspected there was gold in the area, and he was concerned that Muir might "blow his cover." Consequently, Harris waited for Muir and Young to depart before finally settling the claims. Interestingly, John Muir recounts this incident in his book, *Travels in Alaska.* In the book, Muir states his suspicions about these two men's actions. Richard Harris thought he had "pulled the wool over Muir's eyes," but Muir knew what Harris was doing all along. Muir was a naturalist, not a prospector, and most likely wouldn't have revealed knowledge about a gold field even if he had discovered it himself. We will never know!

On October 4, 1880, Harris drew up papers naming the area the "Harris Mining District." Pilz, the grubstaker, required that he receive two of every three claims staked. Following these instructions, Harris staked claims for himself, Juneau, Pilz, and James Carroll, the captain of the steamship, *California.* All together, he staked nineteen placer claims and sixteen lode claims. Harris and Juneau then returned to Fort Wrangell near Sitka with 1,000 pounds of high-grade ore. Their arrival in Wrangell on November 17, 1880, created a colossal stir, and a rush was on to the new Harris Mining District. Dozens of miners stampeded their way to the area to stake their own claims before all the good claims were gone. Little did they know that Pilz had already underhandedly claimed the lion's share for himself.

The United States Mining Act of 1872 declared that five miners must be present to officially establish a mining district. Harris definitely stretched the limits of this ruling when he made his claims with only his name and Juneau's signed on the documents. To complete the required five miner roster, Harris added the names of three Tglingit Indians, calling them miners. In so doing, Harris thought he had neatly sewed up most of the better claims for Pilz and himself in this newly formed mining district. There was a huge uproar about the authenticity of this district, though, and the literacy of Joe Juneau was put to the test of public scrutiny as well.

Within days, the new city of Harrisburg was bursting with miners, prospectors, and loners from every conceivable area of Southeast

Alaska. The new district also attracted its fair share of lawyers, some of whom ultimately made more money than the miners themselves. All the 1880 stampeders needed do in order to reach the gold fields was board a boat and sail up or down the Gastineau Channel between the mainland and Douglas Island and finally disembark at Harrisburg. Not only was there an abundance of gold in the basin above Harrisburg, but there was plenty of gold to be discovered on Douglas Island across the channel. Truly, Harris and Juneau had discovered a gold mine!

By early 1881, this new mining region was bulging with over 150 prospectors. Because of his scheming dealings, Harris was exceedingly unpopular among his colleagues. On February 8, 1881, thirty-one miners met and declared Harris' claim rules null and void, yet they still ratified the location of the claim. Harris' choice of city names—Harrisburg—didn't set well either. In addition to declaring the rules ineffective, the miners voted to rename the town after a popular navy captain who was sent to the area to maintain order, and it became "Rockwell." The United States postmaster, though, refused to comply with this change and continued to call the town Harrisburg, only confusing the situation.

This name change opened an ongoing argument about the town's name which boiled among the miners for several months. On December 12, 1881, another town meeting was called for yet another vote. The general consensus continued to be against Richard Harris' underhanded proxy claims. Joe Juneau took advantage of the situation, and legend has it that the night before that town meeting, Juneau bought generous rounds of drinks for everyone. At the meeting the following day, forty-seven men voted to change the name of Harrisburg to "Juneau City." Eventually the "city" part was dropped, and the town has been Juneau ever since.

It was only because people were unhappy with Richard Harris, that Joe Juneau enjoyed the distinction of having a future capital city named after him, but he never really enjoyed any of the true riches of the gold fields. After his sojourn in the Juneau vicinity, his life followed a rather lackluster, ho-hum pattern. Like dozens of other would be millionaires and prospectors, Juneau wandered from one big claim to another, both in the Canadian Klondike and in other Alaskan strikes. When he died in 1903, his final request was to be buried in Juneau—the town named for him. Today, Juneau's remains rest in the Juneau cemetery alongside scores of other forgotten wanderers and would be millionaires.

Throughout the next thirty years, Juneau's many mines changed hands repeatedly. The Juneau mine fields were rich with colorful characters and human achievements that far superseded the era. The mine that began in Juneau ultimately became the world's largest low grade mine. In the very first year of its existence, it rendered $1,000,000 in gold. The area had several different mines that changed hands repeatedly. Names like George Garsa, George Statler, and Williams Sanders are all part of Juneau's early history. Names of Juneau's early mine can be confusing, too, but the Perseverance Mine came into existence in 1881.

To develop the mines to the degree that was necessary, it was soon evident that major capital backing was needed. Adams and Carter from San Francisco were the first to provide such funds, and in 1888, the Alaska Eastern Mining and Milling Company built the first stamp mill in the area. In 1895 the mine went into receivership, and on Dec. 28 of that same year, a snow slide destroyed the mill. It was such a ferocious slide that the watchman's body wasn't discovered until July 1896.

In 1900 an Englishman named Sutherland renamed the mine the Alaska Perseverance Mining Company. Sutherland's English financial base later caused him major problems, though. Under Sutherland's leadership, a tunnel and the Alexander cross cut were begun. Throughout 1902-1903, they drilled and blasted away at the tunnel, and Sutherland bragged that he would eventually complete a 300 stamp mill and a 10,000 foot tunnel reaching from the mine to the tidewater. In the early days, ore was transported down the mountain with four-horse wagons via Basin Road. Later, a short train was built on the mountain ridge to expedite this process. Despite all his work and all his bragging, by 1907 Sutherland had only twenty stamps in operation. The first year that these stamps were in operation, the mine brought up 32,000 tons of rock, producing $70,000 of gold. Finally, by 1908, 100 stamps were operating in the new mill.

In 1905 Charles Thorndike established a claim above Perseverance Mine and tried to divert the use of water from the established mine to his new B.C. Claim. This situation precipitated a precedent setting lawsuit. Judge James Wickersham, the highly respected judge of the third Judicial Division, ruled in favor of the Perseverance Mine. He ruled that water had more value than gold. This incident merely exemplifies the constant litigations that plagued this region. Most suits dealt with overlapping claims or outstanding money to creditors, but the suit between the Perseverance Mine and the B.C. Claim became precedent setting and remains one of the most important legal decisions of the era.

Under the U.S. territorial act, it was illegal to expand businesses using foreign funds, and the government sued Sutherland for this wrongdoing in 1910. In 1911, then, Sutherland re-formed the mine as the Gastineau Mine. At the same time, he attempted to consolidate his mine with the Nob Gold Mining Company and Silver Creek Mining Company at Sheep Creek across the valley—a consolidation that didn't work. When Sutherland died in England in April 1911, the mine was in disarray. Of its 10,000 shares, Sutherland owned 9,995. To complicate the situation, he also had two wives—one in the United States and one in England.

Enter Mr. Bart Thane: In October 1912, Bart Thane traveled to England and negotiated with Sutherland's English wife to purchase her shares of the Gastineau Mine. At the young age of thirty-three, Thane had already purchased the Grand Hog Mine on the south side of Perseverance. Immediately after he bought the English shares of Sutherland's mine, he merged these two mines.

The first year of joint operation, Thane brought out 300,000 tons of rock and produced $640,000 in gold. Thane rallied $4.5 million from investors and built the newest, most modern mill in the world—one run entirely by electricity. With the installation of electricity, it was at last possible to operate the mill year round. Thane began expanding Sutherland's incomplete tunnels by drilling from the top of the mountain and from the tidewater simultaneously. In April 1914 the two tunnels met at the Alexander cross cut, creating the longest tunnel in the world at that time.

Thane's great start was baptized in reality when his mill burned on Dec. 4, 1912. It was a total loss. He had the youth and gumption, as well as enough financial backers to rebuild—and rebuild he did. He built a company town that rivaled Treadwell across the channel on Douglas Island. It had commodious dormitories, a 400 seat dining room, recreation room, bowling alley, bakery, steam plant, gymnasium, school, library, medical facilities, thirty cottages for married workers, company store, carpenter shop, baseball field, compressor house, and much more. There was even a 730 foot tram to the mountain top to carry the miners back and forth to work.

Eventually a mile and a half long railroad was built to the Silver Creek Mill at the top of the mountain—partially on tailings and the rest on trestles. The train pulled forty carloads of rock at a time, and each car carried fifteen tons. A 42" x 1,000' conveyer belt collected the crushed rocks; then the rocks were sent to a huge cylinder that beat them into even small rocks. From the mountain top ore was funneled from one layer to another until gold was retrieved. The retrieved gold was melted into bars right on site; the rest of the small rocks and powder was shipped to California for further rendering. Nothing was wasted.

The Juneau Mine as it appeared in 1953

Since the mine's gold was low grade ore, only $2.00 in gold per ton was retrieved; this number slid to $1.16 per ton, and finally only sixty-five cents per ton. Thane's dream was fast dwindling, and soon he was hit even harder. When World War I began, he lost twenty-five per cent of his workers almost over night. He made one last attempt to turn his little world and company town into a pulp mill, but an effort to negotiate with the Japanese failed. His tenure as a wealthy Alaskan landowner and employer was over. He died from pneumonia in 1927—alone in New York City.

The mine wasn't a failure, though. It became the foundation on which a thriving city grew. During their heyday, Juneau's mines produced $9,740,500 in gold. Innovative engineering achievements were accomplished as well. In the spring of 1889, a four mile extension was made to Basin Road at a cost of $11,000. This made it easier to get to the mines and established one of the earliest automobile roads in Southeast Alaska. The first generator and air compressor were built by the Juneau Mining and Manufacturing Company in 1892 using the easy accessibility to mountain water falls. This feat made Juneau and its mines the first major region in Alaska to have hydro-electric power.

Juneau Mine in the early 1900s before the trees grew back. Note the railway above the mine and water front below.

Across the narrow Gastineau Channel on Douglas Island, others were searching for gold as well. A Frenchman named Pierre Erussard owed John Treadwell $264.00 for an outstanding freight bill. On September 13, 1881, "French Pete" Erussard ran short of cash, so to fulfill his debt, he simply deeded Treadwell what he thought was a worthless claim. This seemingly simple transaction transformed John Treadwell into a millionaire.

Before he came to Alaska, Treadwell was a twenty year veteran of both placer and lode mines in California and Nevada; he quickly recognized the potential of Erussard's claim. In California, he purchased a five stamp mill and other necessary mine equipment and shipped it all north to Douglas Island. By May 1882, his mine was in full operation and thriving. In 1889 Treadwell sold his interest in the Douglas Island mine for $1.5 million dollars and returned to California. Like many who struck it rich, Treadwell didn't manage his new found riches well. He declared bankruptcy in 1914 and died in New York City in 1927 at the age of eighty-five—a poor man.

The mine that bore Treadwell's name continued to thrive for several years after he sold out, and during those years the company town that bore his name thrived on Douglas Island as well. By 1915 the Treadwell Mine had 960 stamps crushing 5,000 tons of ore a day—a world record! These stamps ran twenty-four hours a day, seven days a week. The noise was so deafening that on Christmas and the Fourth of July—the only days the mine was closed—no one in the town could sleep because it was too quiet.

In its heyday Treadwell had a population larger than Juneau. Treadwell miners were some of Alaska's best paid, receiving wages of $100.00 per month. Employment in the mine automatically qualified miners for membership in the "Treadwell Social Club." This club boasted a marble-lined swimming pool, bowling alley, library, sauna, and Turkish baths. The Treadwell Mine remains Alaska's second largest mine of all time. Between 1881 and 1917, one hundred tons of gold valued at over $25 million were taken from Treadwell.

Initially, when miners from the Treadwell Mine dug beneath Gastineau Channel, they left large pillars of un-mined ore to serve as mine supports; this kept the mine from caving in. By 1916 and 1917, though, the mine was running short of accessible gold ore. These rock pillars also contained gold ore, and in frantic efforts to garner some last gold from the nearly defunct mine, careless miners began "pillar robbing." Knocking down the pillars, however, only weakened their underwater world. By April 21, 1917, the mine was ready to fall in on itself; in a word, it was an accident waiting to happen. A huge sinkhole began below the high tide line of the channel and reappeared on the surface above the mine. When this happened, it swallowed the marble-lined swimming pool of the Treadwell Club. As the tide began coming in, the sinkhole permitted more and more seawater to enter the tunnels, and the mine flooded.

The mine was evacuated while horror-stricken miners stood aghast and watched the sea overtake their livelihoods. In three and a half hours, three million tons of seawater flooded the Treadwell Mine; Alaska's second largest mine was gone forever—just like that. Miraculously, there was no loss of life, but the company town of Treadwell was no more. After the catastrophic cave-in, all three Douglas Island mines closed forever. The island settled into a quiet, sleepy existence. During my years in Juneau, few people lived on the Island, but it still boasted the best—and only—ski bowl in Southeast Alaska.

Juneau boasts other history beside that of the mines. Juneau is Alaska's capital, but that wasn't always so. The history of this capital city is colorful and on-going. After Vitus Bering's ill-fated trip in 1741 opened Alaska to Russian opportunists, the capital was established on Kodiak Island in the Aleutians. In their pursuit of fur pelts, the Russians expanded their Alaskan empire from the Aleutians southward along Alaska's Pacific coast. The village of Sitka on Baranof Island was better suited to navigation, so the Russians moved the capital to Sitka where it remained until Alaska's sale in 1867. For the first nineteen years of American ownership, Alaska's capital was in Sitka. In 1906, however, Congress voted to move the capital to Juneau because it was more accessible to sea traffic north and south along the coast.

Juneau served as Alaska's capital throughout its territorial years. After the gold rush, territorial office work and fishing drove Juneau's economy. When statehood was granted in 1959, the capital remained in Juneau. That same year, though, a reporter from the *Anchorage Daily Times* single handedly began a campaign to relocate the capital. Hardly ever has one man wielded so much influence; the controversy he created continues to this very day. His scheme for this capital move was fortified by some undeniable statistics: Between 1939 and 1950, Juneau's population grew by a mere 2%. During the same period, Fairbanks' population increased 241%, and Anchorage's population increased 658%. It was evident that the bulk of Alaska's population lived in the Anchorage area or the interior. Consequently, a new state capital was proposed to be established between Fairbanks and Anchorage.

After much debate, study, and review, an area north of Palmer called Willow was chosen for the newly proposed state capital. In 1974 Alaskans voted by 57% to move the capital to Willow and create a brand new city. The cost of the move was estimated to be $2.5 billion in 1974, but no definitive plan as to how the money would be generated was ever proposed. Oppositionists jokingly called the project the *Permafrost Brasilia.* To date, nothing specific has happened toward the move, although it has been in and out of courts and on and off ballots ever since. The idea of a different Alaskan capital is likely to stay alive in Alaska for years to come; and, of course, there are varying and heated opinions and passions about the proposed move.

Juneau's prosperity has risen and fallen with different enterprises—lumber and fishing being two. It thrives today on a three-pronged foundation: fishing, government, and tourism. As long as these three indentities stay in tact, its stability is secure.

Alaska's value to national security was firmly established during World War II, the Korean War, and the Cold War. All things considered, statehood seemed to be an inalienable right to Alaska's citizens, and they waged their own war for it. Both transplants from other states and Alaska's Native Americans alike demanded statehood. When Alaska was declared the 49th state in 1959, Juneau was the center of jubilant rejoicing and celebration.

Chapter 12
A House of our Own

Living in a boarding house with three single women is a challenge for any family, and ours was unquestionably no exception. We had no privacy; everything that we did or said was seen by watchful and corrective eyes. The sweet, shy lady who owned the boarding house and her upstairs renter were nice, but still it was tough. Within a few months after we moved in, the mean spirited woman who rented the main floor bedroom moved out. To be perfectly honest; she didn't like us, and the feeling was mutual. None of us missed her criticism or watchful eyes.

Regardless of how nice the other two ladies were, this wasn't our home; we knew it, and they knew it. Every night we shared our evening meal with them, and any attempts at talking about school or situations in the family were monitored by watchful eyes and listening ears. We had no secrets. Our stay in the boarding house was intended to be short-lived—just a few months. But, it didn't work out that way. We ended up living there over a year. That meant that we shared Christmas and holidays and family "fights." Everything was shared and open to observation, second-guessing, and criticism.

It was the tradition in Dad's denomination to hold mid-week prayer services. Both in Fairbanks and Ironton, there were activities on most Wednesday nights geared just for kids. Things were different in Juneau. Since Dad was starting a brand new church from scratch, we had neither a church building nor people to plan kids' programs. Dad rented the American Legion Hall for our Sunday morning and evening services, but there was no where to hold the Wednesday night services.

The boarding house owner came through again and offered her living room for these mid-week meetings. We were trapped. Each Wednesday we hurried through dinner and the dish washing in order to get ready for the prayer service. Mother insisted that everything in the house be neat and tidy; and, of course, all homework and piano practicing had to be done before people arrived as well. Dad's little crowd of parishioners was small on Sunday, but the Wednesday night crowd was even smaller—fifteen people if we were lucky—and that included the three of us kids. We were never allowed to miss. I enjoyed attending church and Sunday school, and even mid-week services for that matter, but I didn't like these meetings in the boarding house one bit. There was nothing for kids. Dad shared a brief Bible lesson; the few people who were there shared prayer requests; and then we knelt for prayer.

Kneeling for prayer is a good thing, but those prayer times were laborious. My escape on Wednesday nights was the overstuffed, velveteen upholstery of the boarding house furniture. When I ran my hand over the fabric, it smoothed out; then, I could draw pictures or write little notes right on the fabric. All I had to do when I finished was run my hand the opposite direction across the fabric and erase what I had just done. The sofa became my own *Etcha Sketch* and my means of survival during those interminable Wednesday night prayer meetings.

Even though I understood that Dad was doing the best he could, my heart ached for companionship and a home of our own. I had school friends, but they went to their own churches. I was hopeful that some girls my age might start attending our church sooner or later. At one Wednesday night prayer service, the adults mentioned an Air Force man who was moving to Juneau with his family and would be attending our church. I got really excited when I heard them say that he had an eighteen-year-old daughter. Eighteen was several years older than I, but it was still closer to my age than nearly everyone else. I was ecstatic; this young woman might be a God send for my loneliness. To my utter disappointment, though, when the family arrived, their daughter was eighteen months old. I had misunderstood, and it broke my heart.

New people of our denomination who were moving to Juneau were always a big interest to Dad. Since our mission was the only one that his denomination had in town, Dad pretty much knew that they would join our little church and be a part of it. And that was true. Even though I was disappointed one time about the new girl's age, one terrific event happened while we were living in the boarding house that had to do with "new" people.

When Dad pastored in Fairbanks, many servicemen came to his church. Mother loved these men and often cooked them Sunday dinner or holiday meals. For years after we left Fairbanks, Mother and Dad stayed in touch with people from all over the United States who had been through the mission there. One young man in particular was from Illinois; he was alone when he arrived—but not for long.

All he could talk about when he got to Fairbanks was "his girl." When "his girl" graduated from high school, she was coming to Alaska to marry him. That's exactly what happened.

When "his girl" graduated from high school, she packed her wedding dress in a suitcase and traveled all the way from Illinois to Fairbanks—alone. Other than her fiancé, she knew no one. Mother and Dad fell in love with these "kids." They had a beautiful wedding in Dad's Fairbanks church, and I was the flower girl. Behind the Fairbanks sanctuary was a one room log cabin which these newlyweds rented and moved in right behind us. They became like family over night. Glen and Shirley were so much in love; they were so cute together and so far from home that everyone loved them—especially Dad and Mom. Before we left Fairbanks, their little son was born and Dad dedicated him.

One day after we were settled in the Juneau boarding house, Dad received a letter from Glen. He was now discharged from the army and back home in Illinois; their family had grown with the addition of a baby girl. Glen was writing to ask Dad if he would hunt for him a job in Juneau. He and Shirley wanted to move back to Alaska with their little family to help Dad start the Juneau church. Our family couldn't believe it. We were SO excited—all five of us. This was like having an older brother or a favorite aunt and uncle move to town.

You better believe that Dad went to work in a hurry to find Glen a job. Glen was a typewriter repairman, and the only office store in town needed someone with his skills. It was a match. Shortly, the deal was settled, and Glen and Shirley were headed our way. Two doors away from the boarding house was a small three-story apartment building. Eventually, Glen and Shirley bought a house in Juneau, but to begin with Dad rented them an apartment in the Seventh Street apartment building. It was all too good to be true. Not only were Glen and Shirley moving to Juneau, but they were going to live next door just like they did in Fairbanks. Once they moved to town, all of us felt more at home in Juneau.

But the situation with the boarding house still loomed over us; it had to change. The tension of day-to-day living was getting to everyone of us—our family and the boarders. After one seemingly interminable year, Dad and Mom knew that something must be done—and soon. Since Dad was pioneering a mission, he was most definitely on a budget. The mission budget allowed enough money for his meager salary as well as funds for rental of the American Legion Hall for Sunday services. Beyond that, there wasn't much; that's why Mother was working full time.

Dad was an extremely hard worker, and his work resulted in a growing congregation, but it was still very small. On a "good" Sunday, there might be fifty people at church, and that included children and babies. Unfortunately, there weren't too many good Sundays attendance wise. This meant that the offerings were small, while the needs were large. Dad's mission board in Kansas City made our little congregation an offer: If we could collect $2,000, they would match it, dollar for dollar.

$2,000 is a drop in the bucket today, but in the mid-fifties, asking Dad's small little flock for $2,000 was like asking for a million dollars nowadays. That's why we stayed so long in the boarding house. It took over a year for Dad's struggling congregation to set aside $2,000 beyond all the other expenses. At last the goal was met, and the promised $2,000 arrived from Kansas City. Now, Dad and Mom had $4,000 to shop for housing. This wasn't much, but it was enough money in those days to buy a modest house in Juneau.

Having enough money and buying an adequate house in Juneau were two different things. Dad's goal was to purchase a lot big enough that eventually there would be room to build a church, so he was looking for a good-sized parcel of level land with a house on it. For weeks Dad and Mom searched. These days, much of the waterfront has been filled in and leveled, but that wasn't the case in the fifties. Nearly everyone in Juneau lived somewhere up or down the side of the mountain. Today, the valley area outside of downtown near Mendenhall Glacier is the most populated section of the city, but in the '50s few people lived there. The congregation that Dad pioneered now has a beautiful church and parsonage in the valley near the glacier. Back when Dad was looking for land, though, there was virtually no level land to be found.

Finally, Dad and Mom found a house they could afford with the $4,000. And, it was on level land! Visitors to Juneau often walk down to the Governor's Mansion. This three story mansion that stands gracefully at the top of Ninth Street hill was built in 1912. Its beautiful white columns and totem poles in its manicured yard are easily visible in Juneau's skyline. Around the corner and up the hill one block from the mansion is the state capitol building. At the bottom of that hill there are three or four small blocks of houses on level land. That's where Dad found a run down house setting on the back of a lot at the bottom of Ninth Street hill—almost in the governor's backyard. It was the epitome of a "fixer-upper." It wasn't much—not at all; but it was ours!

The house had a small front porch that led into a living room that was the full length of one side of the house. The other side of the house had a bedroom at the front, a bathroom in the middle, and a kitchen behind that. Attached to the kitchen was a lean-to porch. There was a doorway between the back of the living room and the kitchen.

The house sat at the back of the lot on the alley. In the living room across from the kitchen was an outside door that led to a side porch. From this porch a stairway led outside and then into to an unfinished basement which consisted of one large room with the furnace in it. Behind the house was a free standing, rickety one-car garage. It was a house in need of much repair before anyone could move in.

People in Alaska are most ingenious when working with housing, and although my Dad wasn't a builder, he and Mom had grand ideas about how to make this place livable for our family. The few men in Dad's congregation who worked with him to get the house livable executed some rather clever modifications—true Alaska style. To begin with, Mother didn't think the kitchen was large enough for cooking and eating, and since there was no dining room, it needed to be enlarged. That's where the little back porch came into play; Dad's helpers knocked the wall out between the kitchen and the porch to make the kitchen bigger. Their idea worked, but it created some definite problems.

There was no insulation on the back side of the kitchen porch which meant that the kitchen was continually cold in winter. Temperatures never dip as low in Juneau as they do in Fairbanks, but Juneau has unbearable winds. They blow across the glaciers and are fierce and biting. As uncomfortable as it was, we could live without insulation since the kitchen had the stove in it. But we couldn't live with the kitchen's slopping floor. Dad and his helpers just could not get it level. Finally, one man had a "temporary" idea. He crawled under the porch with a car jack and jacked up the porch just like you would jack a car to change a tire. Eventually, Dad would get a real builder under the house to shore up the kitchen properly. But, as long as we lived there, that never happened. The jack under the floor kept the house level, and no one ever got around to fixing it. It was comical to walk down the alley and peak under the back of our house and see that it was propped up with a car jack. But this was Alaska, and a "make-do" attitude prevailed.

The next major problem with the house was to find a way to connect the basement with the rest of the house and make it livable at the same time. After much discussion, it was decided that it was too expensive to knock out another wall and unite the two parts of the house. Instead, Mother and Dad made sure that the outside door by the stairs was kept locked at nights for safety, and they concentrated their efforts on finishing the basement. They separated the furnace area with one wall, and divided the rest of the basement in half. This created two good sized bedrooms. There was a small bathroom in the basement which they cleaned up; it didn't have a tub or shower, but there was a stool and a sink.

The two newly created basement bedrooms were for Jason and me; and Dad rigged up a small cot upstairs for Sammy. Mother painted the cinder block walls and made curtains for the tiny windows that were near the ceiling on the ground level. Closets were too expensive to build so Mother ordered cardboard closets from Sears. Looking back, these rooms weren't spectacular; in fact, they were more Spartan than anything else. But, Jason and I didn't notice. After a year in the boarding house, rooms of our own were a dream come true—especially for Jason; those fussy women had driven him ragged. Since we were separated from the rest of the house by an outside wall, it was like being in our own world when Jason and I were down in the basement.

Mother and Dad gutted the living room and completely refinished it. Mother wanted wall-to-wall carpet which was absolutely too expensive for our budget. She was extremely creative, though, and came up with an ingenious plan. From Sears she ordered an over-sized rug. It was a pretty rug with a floral design that I thought was gorgeous. She then had a carpet installer cut the rug to the size of the room and lay it wall-to-wall. Thanks to Mother's clever idea, we had wall-to-wall carpeting. Mother always said, "Where there's a will; there's a way."

The house was renovated, but we still needed furniture. When we left Ironton, Dad sold everything, and all the time we lived at the boarding house, we used the furniture there. The furniture Mom and Dad bought in Juneau wasn't as nice as what they bought in Ironton. They made one big investment when we moved into the "new" house, though; they bought a piano. Now that we were moving out of the boarding house, Jason and I needed a piano of our own for practicing. Our little spinet held a place of honor at the back of the living room on the wall by the basement stairway.

Once the re-modeling was complete, I thought we would move in right away, but Dad had another idea. He decided to host a neighborhood vacation Bible school in the vacant, renovated house. The piano was moved in so that I could be the Bible school pianist, and then Dad had us pass out flyers about the Bible school in our new neighborhood. What fun we had. Several dozen kids came, and for a full week, our new house echoed with the voices of children. The kitchen was used for making *Kool-aid* and cookies, and the basement was used for handcrafts. What a christening to our new mission parsonage.

When that week was over, Dad moved our new furnishings into the house; at last, we had a home of our own after over a year in the boarding house. What a relief it was. Perhaps, though, the most relieved people were the two ladies back at the boarding house. I suspect that our family made a lifelong impression on them both, and I seriously doubt whether another family ever lived there—ever!

The neighborhood Bible school at our house – 1954

There were a few things yet to be done to the house when we moved in. Dad painted the outside and the roof and shored up the rickety garage as much as possible. He intended to paint the house a light yellow and the roof a dark green. Somehow the paint came out different colors than he expected; the house was a bright, yellow, and the roof was dark, dark green. You couldn't miss it as you came down the Ninth Street Hill. Still, our house was a 100% improvement from the way Dad bought it.

Dad's goal was to clean up the garage enough that he could park our car inside in the winter. While he was working on the garage, we had one very memorable day. Under the front eve of the garage, Jason spotted a gigantic wasp nest. It was almost a foot in diameter. Dad's Oklahoma upbringing came to his rescue in getting rid of the nest. He soaked a rag in oil and then lit it. While Jason held a garden hose so that the garage wouldn't catch on fire, Dad burned those wasps out of house and home—without compromising our garage or the house next door.

In addition to the wasp nest, we had one more extremely unforgettable event after we moved into our new house. We quickly discovered that the house had a resident nest of rats! Mother was appalled—as we all were. Rats, mice, and bugs never lived at our house. My mother personified clean and neat and orderly. Regardless of her cleanliness, the rats were there before us, and they were undeterred by our presence. One night when Mother was up late reading, a rat the size of a cat ran right past her feet. That did it! As far as she was concerned, the rats had to go or we'd just move back to the boarding house.

Dad began to pursue those rats with a vengeance. He set traps and waited; nothing happened. The rats were nonplussed and continued running rampant. One morning when we got up, we discovered that they had literally chewed away about an inch on the door between the house and the basement. These were colossal rodents, and we were all scared of them. For days, I was afraid to go to sleep for fear that they would invade my bedroom.

It was Jason who came up with the final solution. He spotted their hole in the front yard by the porch and suggested that Dad back the car up to the hole and pipe carbon monoxide into it. His idea was not only clever, but effective. Dad set traps that night confident that this would be the sure fire solution. The next morning, though, the traps were empty. We were all getting desperate. Mother was serious about her threat to move, and we all were agreeing with her by this time.

Before the day was over, though, we heard Jason shout from the basement. As we were running down the stairs, he was running up the stairs grinning from ear to ear. In his hand he had a shingle with the biggest rat I've ever seen on it—dead! Apparently, just as Jason went into his basement bedroom, the drugged rat staggered across the floor in front of him. He took a baseball bat and finished off that rat in quick order. The rat episode is an ugly memory, but it was painfully real at the time. As it turned out that one huge rat is the only we ever found. For the rest of our days in that house, there were no more unwelcome guests.

Over fifty years later, our little house still stands at the bottom of Ninth Street Hill. Looking at it now, I can't imagine how Dad thought he could put a church *and* a house on that dinky lot. The current owners have built a large enclosed front porch, torn down the old garage, and fenced in the yard, but it's still the same house. These days, however, it's even more weather worn than it was back then, and it looks extremely small. In 1954, however, we were thrilled to have it. It was a home of our own, and it meant two things; our family was alone at last, and Dad's little church was growing—ever so slowly, but it was still growing.

Chapter 13
Shipwrecks & Plane Crashes

Alaska is undoubtedly one of the most picturesque destinations in the world. Altogether it is a land of endless beauty and unfathomable wealth. It has more coastline than all the rest of the United States combined. Within its borders are seventeen of North America's highest mountains. It has countless glaciers, rushing rivers, mountains, streams, and wildlife beyond description.

Its size alone is mind boggling, for it is nearly three times the size of Texas. When a map of Alaska is superimposed on a map of the United States, the Southeastern panhandle reaches Florida; the eastern border touches New England; the western border reaches California; and the Aleutian Islands extend far into the Pacific Ocean. Thousands of square miles are uninhabited; in fact, only one-twentieth of one per cent is inhabited even today. A person can live a lifetime in the state and travel it extensively without ever seeing or experiencing even half of it.

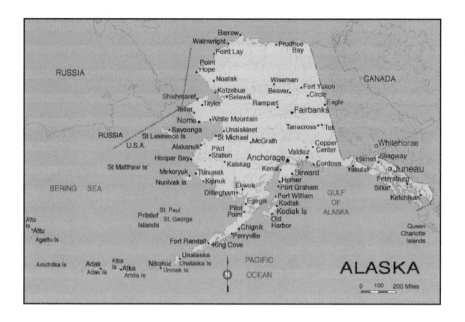

Because of Alaska's vastness and extreme arctic temperatures, the weather is its biggest challenge. It can change in a heartbeat, and it can be brutally harsh. Travel in Southeast Alaska is dependent on water and air; there is virtually no other way to move around. With the exception of Juneau, every town and village in Southeast Alaska is on an island; roads are limited at best and hazardous at worst. Juneau, Southeast Alaska's largest city, has approximately eighty miles of roads—including city streets. Ketchikan is much the same, except that it is situated on an island. Car theft isn't very profitable in Southeast Alaska; there's no way to make a getaway. When an area is dependent on water and air, safety becomes a primary objective. Despite precautions of all kinds, though, there are often catastrophic accidents. Two such catastrophes happened during my tenure in Juneau.

Alaska's history is replete with accounts of shipwrecks. On October 25, 1918, the Canadian steamship *the Princess Sophia* sailed from Skagway loaded to the hilt. It was the last ship to leave the Klondike until spring; consequently, there were several families with children aboard. And, of course, there were thousands of dollars in gold. After the little ship left Skagway and had traveled just a few miles down the Lynn Canal, *the Sophia* ran aground on Vanderbilt Reef. Just like that, it was "high and dry" in the middle of the fjord in a blinding snow storm and tumultuous winds. There were 353 souls aboard.

The Princess Sophia was double hulled, but only the bottom hull was compromised by the hit. Straightaway, an assortment of boats in a variety of sizes and descriptions began to circle the distressed ship. *The Sophia* lowered two or three life boats, but it was quickly apparent that the vicious storm would shatter them on the rocky reef below. That rescue effort was terminated. Next, the captain of *the Sophia* shouted across the waves with a megaphone to the would-be rescuers. Together, *the Sophia* and the rescuers attempted to rig a pulley and basket system to offload the women and children to safety.

Ultimately, the determination was made that *the Sophia* could weather the storm, and the captain opted to keep all passengers aboard. When the tide rose, he decided, his little marooned ship would float off the reef and limp into Juneau less than a hundred miles down the fjord for repairs. Messages were sent ahead to make preparation for this influx of refugees. Dozens of Juneau's residents began preparing rooms and food for the stranded travelers.

Sadly, that's not how it fleshed out. As the storm worsened, the circling rescue ships were forced to seek refuge along the walls of the fjord. With several boats and ships in sight of *the Sophia*, all at once a massive wave caught her bow. In an instant she sank backwards into the deep and frigid fjord. 353 people perished instantly; there was only one survivor—a dog. The sinking of *the Sophia* is still one of the saddest chapters in United States maritime history. It was a catastrophe that didn't need to happen. It has gone nearly unnoticed by the world at large for years because the wreck occurred simultaneously with the ending of World War I and the great flu epidemic of 1918. Nevertheless, the citizens of Juneau never forgot. The city that was to be a haven of refuge became a gruesome, grisly morgue.

One year before we moved to Juneau, our little city came precariously close to repeating the 1918 *Sophia* tragedy. When ships sail into Juneau, they pass huge Admiralty Island and then slip into the Gastineau Channel that separates Juneau and Douglas Island. Gastineau Channel is the remainder of a glacially formed fjord; it's deep enough to sail into, but not deep enough to sail through. Consequently, ships and boats sail into Gastineau Channel, turn around, and then sail out the way they entered. It's that way today, and it's always been that way.

A sister Canadian ship to the ill-fated *Sophia, the Princess Kathleen,* was on its way south from Juneau in September 1952. The captain, the crew, and the passengers enjoyed their stay in Juneau very much like cruise ship passengers do today. The *Red Dog Saloon* has been a Juneau institution for decades, and many passengers from *the Kathleen* visited the world famous saloon that September. Unfortunately, some of the navigational staff spent time at the saloon as well. That was a mistake! When *the Kathleen* departed Juneau that night, it failed to turn around and leave Gastineau Channel the same way it entered. Instead, the little ship proceeded south through the narrow channel. Regardless whether the tide is in or the tide is out, the Gastineau Channel is not navigable—even for large fishing boats.

A few miles south of Juneau near Lena Point, *the Princess Kathleen* ran ashore in the channel's shallow water. When the citizens of Juneau received news of pending disaster virtually in their own backyard, they were not about to allow history to repeat itself in such a catastrophic manner so near their town. Dozens of locals rushed to Lena Point and the site of the sinking vessel Hand over hand and one by one, Juneau's residents rescued 387 souls—every single passenger and crew member of *the Kathleen*. Our boarding house had been one of the many Juneau homes that took in refugees after the 1952 rescue. This little ship that served as a World War II supply ship and survived hostilities off the coast of Malta during the war was brought down in peacetime by a careless captain. What a pity!

The rescue efforts after the sinking of Kathleen

Shortly after we settled in Juneau in 1953—just one year after the disaster—divers began bringing up passengers' possessions as well as other relics and memorabilia from the sunken ship. When items were recovered, they were displayed in downtown store windows. How fascinating it was to peer through department store windows at people's personal possessions, the ship's china, the ship's bell, and numerous other items that the divers retrieved.

One of our favorite places to visit in Juneau was the Shrine of St. Therese, a Catholic retreat center near Lena Point. In the late 1930s, a 400 foot causeway was built across the water to tiny Crow Island, and there a rustic rock chapel was built. The Stations of the Cross are situated around the circumference of the island, now renamed Therese Island. We loved this spot and frequented it many times; its solitude and natural beauty are unmatched. If the tide was just right,

The Princess Kathleen sinking

it was possible to spot the mast of *the Princess Kathleen* from the back side of *St. Therese* still visible above the waters. Now, over fifty years since the shipwreck, *the Princess Kathleen* has crumbled and decayed beneath the sea; no longer is any of it visible. Looking at that lonely mast protruding from the ocean always gave me a chill and reminded me that the waters of Alaska are demanding and have claimed the lives of hundreds of souls through the years.

The story of the sinking of *the Kathleen* had a happy ending for everyone. Everyone but the crew, that is; I certainly would not want to have been in their shoes. There was another incident, though, that happened while we lived in Juneau that impacted my life and still today reminds me of the fragility of life.

The Princess Kathleen ran aground and sank off Lena Point

When my mother searched for a music teacher in Juneau, she found a dilly! Her name was Carol Beery Davis; she and her husband, Travis Davis, were legends in Juneau, and all Alaska for that matter. Mrs. Davis came to Alaska as a young woman, met her husband, and together they stayed and raised a family of four girls. She was both a musician and a poet, although music was her first passion. Mr. Davis was a photographer of some renown. Mrs. Davis began teaching piano in Juneau as a young woman, and over the years taught hundreds of students out of her home on Sixth Street not far from the boarding house. You couldn't go anywhere in the lower forty-eight and find a more qualified or better teacher. She was the absolute best.

Through her energies and passions, Mrs. Davis single-handedly instituted an aggressive concert series in Juneau. She was so respected in the music world that she was able to schedule some of the finest pianists, string players, harpists, and other musicians in the entire world for the Juneau concert series. Because of Mrs. Davis' tireless efforts, Juneau was not lacking in cultural events. During our years there, my parents made certain that we had season tickets to all these concerts.

When she wasn't teaching piano, Mrs. Davis was boating Southeastern Alaskan waters, beach combing, or mountain climbing. These excursions into the wilderness and the waters of Southeast Alaska inspired much of her poetry. At one time, she hired Jason to meet steamships with flyers about her poetry books. To discover one of her poetry books these days is a rare find.

Mrs. Davis taught each of her daughters piano, and each of them also mastered a string instrument—either the violin, cello, or viola. In 1954, two of her daughters (Patte and Sylvia) spent the summer in Juneau; Patte had a summer job with Alaska Fish and Wildlife, and Sylvia was vacationing in the area. Both of these women, as well as the Davis' oldest daughter, Shirley, had already achieved outstanding musical credentials. Sylvia was under contract with the Buffalo Symphony Orchestra, and Patte had just transferred from the Miami University orchestra to Columbia University in New York City to study for a master's degree in music. Their oldest daughter, Shirley, also lived in New York where she played cello in the symphony.

Mrs. Davis scheduled a "Violin and Cello Musicale" featuring two of her outstanding daughters, Sylvia and Patte. The concert was to take place September 12, 1954, at the Twentieth Century Theatre before the girls went back outside in the fall. Everyone in Juneau was enthusiastic about this concert. It would be great. For weeks, the Davis concert was the talk of the town; tickets were sold; the date was set; and many preparations were made for this event that would feature Juneau's own home grown talent.

On September 3, 1954, Patte Davis Bidwell was headed home from a legal hearing in Sitka with four Fish and Wildlife Service co-workers. When their plane failed to arrive in Juneau, no one was very concerned. Fish and Wildlife hadn't been advised of the plane's departure from Sitka, and it was supposed that the party was taking advantage of clear and unlimited visibility to make extensive stream surveys of salmon. Rain in Southeast Alaska is an accepted way of life, so when weather is good, everyone maximizes it.

Somewhere over Admiralty Island near Juneau, though, their Grumman Goose (Appendix # 4) crashed. Rescue evidence and survivor reports indicate that the pilot was attempting to put the small plane down in a meadow when he lost control and a wing sheared off on a pine tree. It is surmised that the plane was attempting to make an emergency landing because of a fuel shortage. Final reports revealed that the Grumman Goose ran out of gas at an altitude of less than

2,000 feet. The glide angle of such a plane without power brings it down at the rate of 3,000 feet per minute.

Alaska Air Crash Is Fatal To Five

Associated Press

Juneau, Alaska, Sept. 3 — Five persons died in the wreckage of a U. S. Fish and Wild Life Service plane which crashed on rugged Admiralty Island, a rescue party reported today from the scene.

a FWS biologist from Seattle, and Patti Birdwell Davis, member of a Juneau family who was working for the service while vacationing here from New York.

Miss Davis was a concert musician who was planning to study for her master's degree in music at Columbia University this fall. She formerly was a member of the Fort Lauderdale Symphony Orchestra and was to join a sister in a concert here in two weeks.

Three died instantly—including Patte Davis. One man burrowed himself out of the wreckage, yet died at the scene as well. The lone survivor was severely injured when he was thrown clear of the smashed plane. Regardless, he managed to stagger two miles down a creek, often wading breast-deep in the water. When he reached Stephens Narrows, he was miraculously spotted by a Fish and Wildlife plane. Luckily, the FWS director was aboard that very plane and immediately sent out word of the sighting. Miraculously, the survivor was rescued. He had broken ribs, deep gashes in his head and body, and an injured hip, yet he was still able to gasp out a rather incoherent location of the wreckage. Volunteers toiled all night and the next day before they reached the bodies and brought them out for burial.

The concert was cancelled, and all Juneau grieved. It was a sad moment in time for the Davis family, but it was a sad time for Juneau as well. A young lady with so much promise and so much local history was gone forever. Travis Davis was a member of the search party that located the plane, and he was the one who took the pictures of the crash that took his daughter's life.

True to their indomitable Alaskan spirit, the Davises rescheduled the concert for one week later—September 20, 1954. Their oldest daughter, Shirley Davis Reed, flew home to Juneau from New York and took her sister's place on the cello. The gowns all three women wore that night were designed and made by Patte Davis earlier that summer. The final encore that Sunday afternoon was Rachmananoff's "In the Silence of the Night," and the Davises dedicated the concert to their sister and daughter, Patte. Proceeds from the concert went to the Patte Davis musician's scholarship fund for a deserving Juneau music student.

September Soiree Set Tomorrow at Theater

Juneau headline for rescheduled Davis concert

I remember that concert on that extraordinary fall Sunday afternoon. The theatre was packed, and Juneau's citizens grieved for one of their own while at the same time delighting in magnificent and ethereal music—music that was brilliantly delivered by Mrs. Davis and her daughters, Sylvia and Shirley. The Patte Davis Memorial Concert was a significant mixture of musical euphoria and family pathos.

Alaska is beautiful, but Alaska is unforgiving, and circumstances can change in an instant. The incidents of *the Kathleen* and the death of Patte Davis underscored that fact of life for me as a young girl. Little did I know in September 1954 that in only three months, I would face my own first personal loss.

Chapter 14
Sunshine Holidays

Southeast Alaska is breathlessly beautiful; "if" you can see it. Its countless mountains and endless waterways, deep fjords and ancient glaciers, and rugged wilderness areas make it a tourist's delight and a sportsman's paradise. Southeast Alaska is located in the world's largest temperate "rain forest," a term that tourists and cruisers find odd. Generally, people think of a rain forest as a hot, steamy jungle in South America. Visitors are often shocked by Southeast Alaska's rainy weather—even in summer. It rains and rains, and then it rains some more. Southeast Alaska's weather can be anyone's guess, and it can change radically from hour to hour.

Southeast Alaskans are acclimated to this exceptional weather: rainy weather is a way of life. It's easy to distinguish visitors from residents in Southeast Alaska; residents seldom use umbrellas. The region's rainfall measurements are staggering: Ketchikan comes in first with over thirteen feet of rain and nearly three feet of snow yearly. It rained more in Juneau when we lived there, but since then recent global climatic changes have reduced its annual rainfall greatly.

Juneau now gets four and a half feet of rain and nearly nine feet of snow yearly. Even though Southeast Alaska's residents are accustomed to the dreary, incessant rain, it can still be depressing when it rains day after endless dark day.

When the sun comes out, there is no place more beautiful or more inspiring than Southeast Alaska. Juneau's offices and schools have a perfect solution to the phenomenon called sunshine. After it has rained day upon endless day and when the sun finally comes out, Juneau's schools and state offices declare a "Sunshine Holiday." It usually happens mid-day. When it appears as though the sun is going to stay out for a few hours, those in authority get on P.A. systems and tell everyone to go home and not come back for the rest of the day. Even Alaska's governor has been known to declare a "Sunshine Holiday." No one needs to be told twice. On these holidays, Juneau looks as though it were turned inside out. No one is indoors; everyone is outside.

Our family was no different than any other. After weeks of endless rain, we nearly lived for a sunshine holiday. On those rare days, Mother came home from her office and packed a lunch; then we took off for the glacier or the mountains. Sunshine holidays were glorious, but they were few and far between. It didn't take us long to realize that if we waited for a sunshine holiday, we would miss most of the region's natural beauty. Like everyone else in Juneau, we picnicked and hiked dozens of hours in the rain. Even picnics that began on sunny days often ended up in the rain under a shelter. That's life in the rain forest.

Juneau is situated in the middle of the Tongass National Forest and the Juneau Ice Field. Tongass National Forest is the nation's largest, and it stretches from the village of Yakutak in the north to south of Ketchikan and encompasses 16.9 million acres. There are thirty-eight major glaciers within Juneau Ice Field's 5,000 square miles, including Taku, Herbert, and Lemon. Just thirteen miles from downtown Juneau is Mendenhall Glacier—one of the world's most visited natural attractions. Whichever direction you travel near Juneau—whether by land, air, or sea— you will encounter a glacier. These glaciers are historic and beautiful and stretch the imagination of visitors and locals alike, but they are cold—even in summer. In summer it's fun to hike on and around the glaciers, but wintertime is a different story.

When we lived in Alaska's Interior, we endured brutal cold. It was common for the mercury to drop below fifty degrees and hover there for days. One winter in Fairbanks, it dropped to sixty-three below, and one day on our Alcan Highway trip of February 1950 (*Little House in the Arctic*, chapter 10) it was seventy-five below zero. That's cold! The cold in Alaska's Interior is a dry cold; it never feels as cold as it really is. People who fail to show proper respect for this cold have been permanently deceived and even injured by it; it is indeed unforgiving and deceptive.

When we moved to Southeast Alaska, Dad and Mother studied the region's temperature patterns. We were all relieved to discover that it didn't get anywhere near as cold in the Southeast as it does in the Interior. Our first winter in Juneau, though, we learned a great deal about glacial winds and how they significantly impact the "chill factor." When comparing Southeast Alaska's winter temperatures to temperatures in the Interior, you must take the winds into account for it to be a true comparison.

High in the snow-capped mountains, winds follow the descending pathways of the glaciers as they meander and find their inexorable pathways toward the sea below. As winds move across the glaciers, they pick up both velocity and intensity. The air chills measurably; the wind is relentless and becomes vicious and bitterly cold. We soon learned that winters in Southeast Alaska can "feel" much colder than those in the Interior. When Juneau's weatherman reported that a "Taku wind" was on its way, Juneau's residents hunkered down. A Taku wind announcement was due warning that fierce winds were blowing across the glaciers, and we knew instantly that it would be bitterly cold. Wind velocities, coupled with sub-zero temperatures, create biting and brutal conditions.

It was mid-August 1953 when we arrived in Juneau, and the brief summer was nearly over. Shortly, we were introduced to weather that we could have never imagined in the Interior. It wasn't so much a culture shock to move to Juneau; it was a "weather" shock. Fifty years later, I still have vivid and miserable memories of the incessant rain and the bitter winds. My brothers and I only walked down the mountain two blocks from the boarding house to the Fifth Street School, but I recall being absolutely chilled to the bone by the time I got to school, or by the time I got back home again.

When we moved to the house at the bottom of Ninth Street Hill and I was a grown-up seventh grader, I refused to wear proper winter gear to school. In the early fifties it was fashionable for girls to wear pleated skirts and bobby socks. I was too old, I thought, to wear snow pants under my skirts. Mother didn't think so and insisted that I wear them. More than once, I remember leaving the house, taking off my snow pants, and carrying them to school so that I would "look" like the other girls. All of us girls were doing the same thing. Peer pressure is "big" with middle school kids, and I guess it wasn't any different then than it is now.

During the years we lived in Juneau, our family was on an exceedingly tight budget. Jason and I learned to ice skate in Fairbanks, but we had long since outgrown our skates. Mother and Dad didn't have extra money to buy skates; so skating was out. There was great skiing at the Douglas ski bowl across the channel on the island, but we didn't have money for skis and ski gear either. Someone gave us a couple of sleds; so whenever it snowed, we did a lot of sledding—especially when we moved to the bottom of the Ninth Street Hill. That was, indeed, a "world class" sledding hill.

Even though we didn't have money to engage in expensive winter sports, hiking was free, and we did a lot of it. When ships dock in Juneau these days, the first thing passengers see is the Mt. Roberts Tramway. This modern tram, completed by the Tglingit Indians and the Goldbelt Corp. in August 1996, whisks riders in a beautiful gondola 1,800 feet up the mountain in less than ten minutes. It's a beautiful ride, and once you reach its end, you can visit the Chilkat Theater, a bar and grill, a gift shop, and impressive displays of Native American artwork. In addition, there is a nature center that provides trail maps for hikers who choose to continue hiking. The Mount Roberts Tram carries over 200,000 visitors to the mountaintop each season and is now one of Southeast Alaska's most frequented tourist attractions. It's an absolute breeze to get to the top of Mt. Roberts, but it wasn't always this way.

The trail head to Mt. Roberts begins on Sixth Street just one block down the mountain from the Seventh Street boarding house. Many days—in rain or shine—we headed up the trail toward the top of the mountain. Sometimes we'd hike as far as the timber line; sometimes we'd go all the way to the top; and sometimes we would go as far as weather or time allowed and then return home. It was that simple—only one block from home was the trail head to a world famous mountain trail.

Our family became reasonably knowledgeable about mountain plants, trees, and flowers. I especially loved the large, lush ferns. You must experience them in their unspeakable abundance to fully fathom their magnificence. One plant that we learned to avoid was the devil's club. This plant has an unmistakable presence. It has leaves like palm fronds, spines under the leaves and on the stalks like daggers, and red berries that are candy for bears. Its leaves with their tiny little thistles can tear you up in a flash. We never wanted to tangle with a devil's club. Interestingly, Tglingit Indians have used the devil's club for years as a deterrent to many diseases. In fact; the "Tglingit aspirin" has been approved by the Food and Drug Administration.

The city park was about four blocks in the opposite direction from the boarding house. We referred to the park as "The Bowl;" today it's called Cope Park. Glaciers create unique geological configurations, one of which is a *kettle*. A kettle is a small lake formed when a glacier retreats and leaves a mass of ice in a glacially sculpted bowl. Over centuries the ice melts, creating lakes of varying sizes. When these lakes go dry, they leave huge bowls carved into the mountains. Such was our city park.

"The Bowl" (aka Cope Park) was a huge three sided bowl created by a glacial kettle. This bowl held picnic tables and shelters, a tennis court that doubled as a winter ice skating rink, hiking trails, and even a swimming pool. Around the top rim of three sides of The Bowl were private homes, while the fourth side opened toward the sea. If you knew where to begin, you could literally sled from the top of The Bowl to the bottom, a distance of several hundred feet and at nearly a ninety degree incline. Roaring and cascading through the middle of The

Bowl is historic Gold Creek. Everyone in town used The Bowl; it is a rustic wilderness setting smack dab in the middle of town, and it was a common gathering place for picnics and parties. After we moved to the house at the bottom of the hill, I often took *Kool-Aid* in a jar, a peanut butter sandwich, and a book to the park. I would hop and jump across the roaring creek until I found a boulder in the sun. There I would eat my lunch and read my book. No finer library has there ever been.

One beautiful sunshiny Sunday some stateside visitors attended our little mission. Visitors and sunshiny days were both rare and anticipated delights; this was a good day! Our visitors had two boys near the ages of Jason and me, and we invited them to go with us to The Bowl for a picnic. While Mother was getting the food together, the four of us kids took a hike. We crossed a small foot bridge spanning Gold Creek, ventured briefly into a mountain cave, and then began hiking up the opposite side of the creek. Gold Creek is ferocious and can be deadly as it roars and rushes down the mountain over and around giant salt and pepper granite boulders—some as big as a small car.

It was such a beautiful day, and we were having so much fun that we soon were a sizable distance into the mountain wilderness and away from the foot bridge. That wasn't a problem, we thought; we'd just find a place in the creek where we could jump from rock to rock, get to the other side, and return to the picnic. Whenever we thought we had a good crossing spot, though, it never worked out. We couldn't quite make it all the way across; someone would "chicken out" in the middle of the creek; or it was too far to jump from one rock to the next.

No one was very concerned. Each time it was too hard to cross, we just turned around in the middle of the creek, went back to the bank, and continued climbing the mountain until we thought we had another good crossing spot. This went on for a long time until we became anxious. We weren't concerned about crossing the creek, because we knew that if it became necessary, we could always retrace our path and cross the foot bridge where we began. None of us had a watch, yet we knew we had been gone far too long; everyone would be looking for us by now. The boys with us didn't know our mother, but Jason and I did. Mother didn't like for us to be late, and she would be unhappy to say the least.

Time—not the creek—was now our enemy. There wasn't time to return to the bridge, and it was imperative that we get to the picnic *post haste*. Far up the mountain we spotted it. Looking back with the objectivity of maturity, I can't believe that any of us even entertained a thought of what we did next, but we did. High in the mountains a small pipe from one of the old gold mines spanned the creek. This pipe was less than a foot in diameter; it was supported by two-by-fours on either side and suspended twenty feet or more above the rushing water and the gigantic rocks. On either side of the creek was a pole about the size of a telephone pole with foot rungs ascending to the top. The whole setup was rickety and old, and long forgotten and unused.

This pipe, we foolishly determined, was our escape mechanism. Even now, I shutter as I think of what we did. One by one we climbed the tall pole on our side of the creek. Then again, one by one, we hunkered down, hugged the pipe, and shimmied across the creek. Suspended high above the ferocious waters and deadly rocks, I wondered what in the world I had gotten myself into as I looked down on potential disaster below. Once across the creek, each of us climbed down the opposite pole until all four of us made it to safety on The Bowl side of the creek where our parents were. We wandered into the picnic late, but sworn to silence. I'm not sure about the boys with us, but Jason and I both knew that what we had just done was dangerously foolish. We were lucky to be back alive. Mother was upset enough that we were late; she didn't ever need to know how perilously close to harm and even potential death we had just been.

Even though we enjoyed The Bowl and frequented it often, the place that our family liked to visit most was Mendenhall Glacier. This famous glacier is thirteen miles from town, stretches a mile and a half across a small lake, and reaches twelve miles into the mountains where it originates. John Muir named the glacier Auk Glacier after a local Tlingit village. *Auk* means *lake* in the Tglingit language, so today's nearby Auk Lake is jokingly called "Lake Lake" by the locals. In 1892 it was renamed Mendenhall Glacier after Thomas C. Mendenhall, superintendent of the U. S. Coast and Geodetic Survey. Many buildings, streets, and businesses in Juneau bear his name as well, but ironically, Mendenhall never visited any place in Alaska.

Like many of Alaska's glaciers, Mendenhall has been retreating since the mid 1700s. Before 1750, its snout reached two miles farther down the valley, and geologists believe that at one time the glacier was a tidal glacier that met the sea. Mendenhall's glacial ice is between 400 and 800 feet thick. It takes the ice at the glacier's face approximately 250 years to flow from the distant ice field to the glacier's present terminus in small Mendenhall Lake.

The glacier that tourists see today looks much different from the glacier my family hiked around. Near the present day visitors' center, there was a trail built twenty years earlier by Depression Era Civilian Conservation Corps workers. The huge, rushing Nugget Falls that is so dominant now wasn't visible when I was a girl. At the site of the falls, we could only see bubbling water coming from beneath the glacier. No one knew then that the bubbling water was really a magnificent waterfall. Not only was Nugget Falls covered by ice in the 1950s, but the location of today's visitor's center and the mammoth land and rock formation that extends into the middle of the lake were both buried by ice as well. The site of today's parking lot was even ice-covered in the 1950s.

My family spent countless hours on beautiful summer nights hiking by the Mendenhall Glacier. Since Mother worked an eight hour day, we would wait for her to get off work and then head straight for the glacier. Summer nights in Alaska are long, and sometimes we would hike until midnight and then by the light of the moon. Generally, we hiked up the side near the present day visitor center, but occasionally we hiked the other side as well. Once we moved to the house at the bottom of the Ninth Street Hill, Mother and Dad let us get a little cocker spaniel. The dog always accompanied us on our glacier and mountain hikes.

Jason and I often got far ahead of Mom, Dad, and Sammy on our hikes. These hikes were aggressive; the trails climbed steep inclines and crossed over numerous waterfalls. The trails were primitive when they were constructed during the '30s, and during the war years they had been neglected. Consequently, sometimes the trail itself was missing or difficult to find. We never got lost, though, but our poor little dog sure had a rough time. In her efforts to keep us together, she would spend some time with Jason and me and then run back to the other three. She did this so many times on a hike that she probably went twice as far as the rest of us. In addition to the threat from devil's club and the ruggedness of the trail itself, there were other potential hiking hazards. More than once Mom and Dad came across steaming bear scat in the trail that Jason and I had just passed. Regardless, we never once saw a bear up close and personal.

In August and September, the streams near the glacier are so thick with spawning salmon that we couldn't even wade through a shallow six inch deep stream. One day while we were picnicking at the glacier, I witnessed nature at work before my eyes in the silty glacial streams. The salmon in this little stream had fought their way back "home;" now, after a journey of several thousand miles, they were nearly dead. Salmon change shape when they spawn and become frightening to behold. It fascinated me to see fish take huge bites out of one another and still keep right on swimming with half their body missing.

Once or twice during our three years in Juneau we made a trek to Herbert Glacier. Even today, this glacier is difficult to reach, but it was especially challenging then. Reaching Herbert Glacier was an experience in itself. Dad drove to the end of the road where a posted sign said, "No cars beyond this point." From there the road became two deep ruts through the forest. Dad continued driving past the sign and down the rutted path. There was underbrush on each side and sometimes over the top of the car. On that road I saw some of the biggest devil's club I've ever seen—some twelve feet or higher. On that road, our car even "high-centered" when the bottom scraped the ground. Eventually, though, Dad reached an open spot on the banks of the Herbert River.

The glacier was on the other side of the river, and there was no way to get a car across. Only a one-man ferry spanned that icy river. One by one, each of us climbed into a bucket like contraption and pulled ourselves hand over hand across the river. The foot trail continued on the other side of the river, and we hiked on to the glacier from there. It was a beautiful glacier to behold, but in this case, "the journey was definitely the destination." Just reaching Herbert Glacier created a life-long memory.

We had one other favorite hiking place. Two blocks from the boarding house, the road takes a turn, and in a flash you are in the wilderness on Basin Road—the road built for gold miners in the 1880s. Basin Road is nearly the same today as it has been for over one hundred years. After you cross a one lane wooden bridge at the end of Gold and Eighth Streets, you are smack dab in a mountain wilderness, yet only six blocks from town. On the left side of the road, Gold Creek rushes wildly down the mountain; at road's end are abandoned mine shafts. When we hiked Basin Road, there were still visible signs of an old hotel hanging precariously on the mountainside. These remains have long since deteriorated.

The historic Treadwell Mine blowout on Douglas Island known as the "Glory Hole" is well-documented. Old-timers in Juneau told us about another little remembered glory hole near Basin Road. With just a few clues as to its location, we decided to go looking for this other "Glory Hole." Half way up Basin Road, we turned to the right and cut through the forest. We were persistent, even though we had to fight tangled underbrush and huge mosquitoes. We crossed several small creeks, even tottering and balancing our way across one of them on a small log. Our efforts were ultimately rewarded. After struggling through the brush for several hundred yards, there it was. On the back side of Mt. Roberts, we spotted a huge gaping cavern approximately the size of a half city block. Descending to the bottom was a rickety mine shaft. I wanted to climb down, but that was definitely "out."

Gramma visited us one summer, and we took her everywhere we had ever been in the whole area, but she enjoyed the Basin Road Glory Hole most. When we left home that day, it was beautiful and sunshiny. The sunshine quickly melted, and we returned home in a drenching rain. Gramma loved to sing. She got a big kick that day out of singing, "I love to go a wandering, along the mountain path." I can still hear "Valdarie, Valdarah" echoing through my memory.

One day three of my friends and I got an old cigar box from the local drugstore. In this box we each placed a special personal "treasure." Together we hiked up Basin Road and hunted through the underbrush until we discovered a beautiful little meadow. It was breathtaking with its lush green ferns, cattails, wild irises, and quiet stillness. In our "secret meadow" we conducted a little ceremony and buried the cigar box; each of us vowing that one day we would return and dig up our treasures. That return trip to the secret meadow, of course, never happened, yet I think I can honestly proclaim that I was one of the very first "Ya Ya Sisters."

One Saturday Mother decided that she and I needed a day together—just the two of us and no one else. Our mother/daughter day was definitely executed Alaska style. Early that morning we packed a lunch and drove across the Juneau/Douglas Bridge to Douglas Island. Once on the island, we proceeded to the head of the ski trail. In those days, there wasn't a road to the ski bowl. Only a small motorized vehicle called the "Oola" built especially for mountain traveling took skiers to the bowl. This tiny sled mobile was built on skis of its own with a cab that seated ten people.

We didn't ski, but this was our wonderful day. When we arrived at the ski bowl, I had never seen anything like it. There were only rope tows, but that didn't stop skiers from tugging their way up the mountain and then sailing down again. Mother and I spent our day on the mountain in a little warming hut built for skiers. We ate lunch, watched the skiers for several hours, and then retraced our way down the mountain in the "Oola." It was years after that before I learned to ski, but that day at the Douglas bowl planted a seed in my heart for the sport.

We never had much money while we were in Juneau, and there was very little sunshine. There are only a few miles of roads in the entire area, but on Sunday afternoons we always took a ride, either to the glacier, out to Thane, to Lena Point and the Shrine of St. Therese, or across to Douglas Island. Mother and Dad loved to sing, and they sang together beautifully. On those famous family rides, they sang and sang, and we sang along with them. Whether it was a sunshine holiday or a typical rainy day, nothing stopped our family from enjoying Juneau's breathless beauty.

Within less than a day's journey from Juneau is Glacier Bay, and a few miles beyond that is the spectacular Hubbard Glacier. Even though we were that close; regretfully, we never visited them. We never even visited Skagway, the historic Gold Rush town less than a hundred miles away. People spend thousands of dollars and travel hundreds of miles from every country in the world to experience what virtually lay in our backyard. On Dad's meager income, we simply did not have the money to visit these places. Lack of funds, though, couldn't stop us from hiking the trails and glaciers in and around Juneau. Looking back, it would have been nice to visit Glacier Bay, for example, so that I could compare it with what is there today, but that just didn't happen. Nevertheless, our years in Juneau gave us all a love and appreciation for the back country and all its secrets.

Chapter 15
Tragedy Close to Home

After living in the boarding house for so long, my brothers and I longed for "normal" family life—whatever that is. When we lived in Fairbanks, we begged for a dog, but when you're cooped up inside nine months a year, a dog isn't all that reasonable. We hardly stayed in Ohio long enough to unpack—much less get a dog. Once we moved to the house at the bottom of Ninth Street Hill, Mother and Dad were out of reasons why we couldn't have a dog and eventually succumbed to our begging and got us a little blond cocker spaniel. We loved that dog and named him "Sparky."

The boys liked Sparky, but I loved him; we were best friends, and he was my constant companion. On nice days when I played outside or rode my bike, he was always right there with me; he even slept at the foot of my bed. Because of the configuration of the hill, three streets converged at our corner beside a big lilac bush. Our old house is fenced today, but in 1954 it was open to three sides. We liked it that way because the lot was so small that the openness made it look and feel bigger.

One afternoon while I was practicing, Sparky got outside somehow. I didn't know anything was amiss until I heard slamming brakes and the yapping of a dog. I recognized Sparky's yelp and was outside as quick as a bullet. On the corner right in front of my house, the milkman had hit Sparky. My little dog only lived a few minutes, and then he was gone forever. I was brokenhearted. How could this happen? Was it my fault? I asked all the questions any grieving person asks after a loss. No answers that my parents gave could sooth my despondency, sense of loss, and wounded spirit. This was my very first encounter with death, and it stung.

Finally, Mom and Dad decided that the only answer for my misery and depression was to get another dog. Sparky was a male, but this time they found a little blond female cocker. No dog could replace Sparky, but it was love at first sight for the three of us and our new dog, Blondie. She was the sweetest dog ever, and she became our hiking companion as we explored the glaciers and trails around Juneau. One year Blondie had pups—nine of them. No one could imagine how such a little dog could have so many puppies, but there they were—nine tiny little balls of fur.

Blondie was too small to nurse all those pups, but nature solved her dilemma. Three of the puppies were born diseased. The vet told Dad that the sick pups must be destroyed; otherwise, all the other pups would be affected and die. One day Dad took the three sick puppies and left; he was gone a long time. When he returned, he didn't have the puppies, but he was melancholy and quiet. We never asked him how he got rid of the pups, but it must have been extremely difficult for him. The six remaining pups thrived, and eventually we gave them all away. Sadly for all of us, we had to leave Blondie behind when we left Alaska a year later. Blondie was great, but I never forgot Sparky. Losing him was an introduction to the reality and fragility of life. What happened later that year affected my young life forever.

The Christmas of 1954 was a wonderful time for our family. That was the year that Mom and Dad bought the latest home entertainment device—a high fidelity record player; we called it a Hi-Fi. Not only did we have a home of our own for the first time in over a year, but our adopted brother, George, came from Tennessee to spend the holidays with us. He wasn't really adopted, but Mom and Dad still called him their oldest son.

George was one of the hundreds of young men who came to Alaska to make a fortune working in construction. He visited Dad's mission in Fairbanks one summer and won my parents' hearts. He was a Southern gentleman if I ever knew one, and he's still a part of our family today. That Christmas, George brought me one of the newest gadgets for a gift; I was one of the first girls in my class to have one. Wrapped beautifully in a cute little box, and laying on a velvet cushion, he presented me with my very own ball point pen. In 1954 ball point pens were as new as the Hi-Fi. Technology was coming to Juneau, and I had my very own ball point pen to prove it. George only stayed with us a few days, and then he flew back to the states before the school holidays were over.

After George left, the three of us were home alone. During the week between Christmas and New Year's of 1954, Juneau had a picturesque snowfall. Ninth Street Hill was the best sledding hill in Juneau—hands down. Once you left the Governor's Mansion at the top of the hill, the street took a sharp turn and came straight down into our yard. Where the street made its turn, we kids piled up snow until there was a large mound of ice at the curve. Then, we started

our descent above the mound, picked up speed, and flew through the
air across the mound. It was hilarious fun.

One day at the end of December, the hill was alive with kids
and sleds. Sammy and I were getting dressed to go outside to sled
when the phone rang. Two of my friends were calling from the other
side of town; they had spent the night together and wanted me to come
over and sled with them. I loved both of them and really wanted to go,
but I first had to get permission. I called Mother at work and asked
if I could go to my friend's house. Her answer was, "No." There was
no one to take me, she explained, and I also had to watch Sammy.
"Besides that," she said, "Ninth Street Hill is the best sledding hill
in town. Go outside right there at home and enjoy the day." I was
disappointed because I wanted to play with my friends, and for a few
minutes I pouted. On such a day, however, I couldn't' sulk too long,
so I got hold of myself, took Sammy, and went outside to sled. It was
so much fun that I quickly forgot my disappointment.

We were thoroughly enjoyed the day. Children coasted down
the hill on their sleds, shot straight over the icy mound, then trudged
back to the top of the hill, dragging their sleds for yet another run. It
was a typical day on a sledding hill; there was a lot of laughter and
jostling for place in line. Everyone, it seemed, eventually ended up in
our yard at the bottom of the hill. Shortly, we began to hear the names
of my two friends; Margaret and Martha. They were on another hill;
why we people talking about them?

Word passed from one kid to another and another, until we
all knew that something out of the ordinary was happening. Without
many words, we drug our sleds quietly off the hill and headed home.
The hill was almost instantly vacant, as though some silent magnetic
force was compelling us to leave. Within minutes Ninth Street Hill was

silent and void of sledders. All the laughing and boisterous behavior was replaced with an ominous silence. No one knew for sure what had happened on the other side of town. The air was heavy, but no one knew why.

Fearfully, I took Sammy and went inside. It was eerie. Margaret and Martha were two of my best friends. All of us took piano lessons from Mrs. Davis; in addition, Margaret was a budding young violinist. I suppose Mrs. Davis really liked that since all of her own daughters were such accomplished string players. There was always a subtle competition among those of us who took lessons from Mrs. Davis to be the last performer at the recital. It was unspoken, but everyone knew that whoever played the last number was the best in Mrs. Davis' eyes. Margaret had performed last at our most recent recital.

We were taught two cardinal rules about sled safety: never be pulled behind a car, and never ride a sled downhill with one person on top of the other. One person sitting behind another was okay, but it was taboo to ride on top of someone. Margaret and Martha were having as much fun on their hill as we were on ours, but they were taking turns riding on top of each other as they slid down their hill. When it was all over, it didn't matter whose idea it was; both girls broke the rule. News travels fast in a small town. Inside the house, I turned on the radio. The announcer was already giving sketchy details of a freak sledding accident.

It was Martha's turn to be on top, and Margaret was lying on the sled. Near the bottom of a steep hill as they were turning their sled into Margaret's front yard, it went out of control. They crashed headlong into a telephone pole in Margaret's yard with everyone watching—including her parents. The impact was so severe that

Martha shot straight up in the air and came right back down again hitting Margaret with full force. The impact displaced Margaret's liver and did other internal damage as well. Dr. Whiteman was called to their home; when he realized the severity of her condition, he rushed Margaret to St. Ann's Hospital emergency room. Surgery was performed, and she received several blood transfusions from frantic local donors. Despite all these efforts, my friend lived only six hours after the accident. Just like that, at 9:25 PM one of my best friends was dead from a senseless tragedy.

In my confused state, I had to do something rather than just lie on my bed and cry. I put a stack of seventy-eight records on our modern Hi-Fi record player, but I didn't pay much attention to the specific records I put on the turnstile. As the records played on and on, I stared out the window at the vacant hill. In a few brief hours, my life turned from fun and innocence to sadness and confusion. As I stared at the empty, snow-covered hill, lively Strauss waltzes droned away on the Hi-Fi.

Wednesday, December 29, 1954, was a tragic and sobering day for the citizens of Juneau. No one had ever experienced anything like this. It was over-whelming. Margaret was buried in the states, but there was a local memorial for her. I'll always remember the day that a dozen of us sixth grade girls left the

Weather Forecast
Fair and cold with low near 6 in Juneau and as low as 16-below in outlying areas tonight. Increasing cloudiness and not so cold with high about 15 Thursday. Occasional gusty NE winds.

THE

VOL. LXXXV., NO. 12,920

Sledding Mishap
Is Fatal to Girl

11-YEAR-OLD DAUGHTER OF FORESTER DIES

Correspondent Says—
CAB Makes 5 Decisions

December 29, 1954 headline

Fifth Street School and walked down the hill to the little Methodist church on the corner for her memorial. The whole episode was numbing. This sort of thing wasn't supposed to happen to me or my friends; we were young and had our entire lives ahead of us. A month earlier, about a dozen of us girls had been to Margaret's house for her birthday slumber party. Now she was gone forever. While the pastor tried to make some sense out of Margaret's death, we wept together for our loss.

It's been over fifty years since that winter day on the hill in Juneau. Now and again I catch a phrase of a Strauss waltz. I may be on an elevator or in a large crowd, but for one brief moment I travel alone to a distant place. Strauss waltzes always remind me of that winter day so long ago. Once again I'm a little girl facing death square in the face. I grew up quite a bit between Christmas and New Year's of 1954. Margaret's death was a life changer for me. Three more times before I was twenty-one, I lost a friend my age in a tragic incident of one kind or another. Each time I lost another friend, I again remembered Margaret and what a loss her death was to all of us young girls in Juneau.

That tragedy touched all our lives closely, and none of us could imagine that within the year death would come perilously close once again. Where death struck next was a shock to everyone in town; it shook all of us to the core. Mother loved her job working for the Territory of Alaska. She got along well with the five other women in her office, and she even eventually adapted to being watched by her boss in the glass office. We were all thankful for her job, because without it, we wouldn't have survived in Juneau.

Sept. 14, 1955, was a normal day for Juneau. It was normal, that is, until 10:30 AM, and then everything went awry. As Mother sat at her desk working, she heard a pop and then a thud coming from an office on the second floor above hers. This was odd, and no one could make any sense of it. Almost simultaneously with the pop and thud there was a great deal of commotion in the entire building. Mother's boss ran out of his glass office and locked the door to the main hallway. Something was amiss, but no one had a clue what it was.

Above Mother's office was the Department of Health. A disgruntled welfare recipient and tuberculosis patient named Lester Mangle decided to take retribution against the territory. He felt that he hadn't received proper treatment because of graft and corruption in the Health Department *and* in Mother's office, the Department of Welfare. He later told police that he thought the Health Department was worse, and that's the only reason he went to the second floor office, rather than to Mother's first floor office. When the bank foreclosed on his home, Mr. Mangle snapped. That was the catalyst that pushed him over the edge and caused him to follow through with his crazed plan to show the world how poorly he felt these two departments had treated him.

September 14, 1955 headline

Mr. Mangle had been plotting his crime of retribution for over a year; it was crazy, but it was clever. He entered the building with a sawed off 30.06 rifle under his coat in a sling which he had devised to conceal the weapon. The sling was made from a curved curtain rod that he wrapped around his shoulders and strapped to his body with a clothesline. The gun was concealed beneath his coat in such a way that he could swing it around and shoot. Unnoticed, he rode the elevator to the second floor, walked the entire length of the hall, opened the door to Room 214 of the Department of Health, and shot and killed the first person he saw—a woman named Elizabeth Cornell. He had never even met Mrs. Cornell nor anyone in the entire building. Once he shot Mrs. Cornell, he laid his gun on the desk, turned to her colleagues and said, "That's right, call the police before I shoot someone else."

He was immediately arrested, and as the police questioned him, he showed no remorse whatsoever. In fact, he acted proud of his dastardly deed. Because this was a territorial office, the case was handed over to a federal court and judge. Two days later, Mr. Mangle appeared before a grand jury and was charged with first degree murder and a federal offense. The jury and the police returned with him to the scene of the crime, where he casually re-enacted the killing for them as though he were demonstrating something outstanding. Investigators noted that he seemed to delight in telling them what he had done and precisely how he did it. It was a cold, heartless action enacted by a crazed man.

The shooting at Mother's office building was the talk of Juneau and the whole territory for weeks. It was so sad and so frightening. I can't even imagine what the news of Mrs. Cornell's senseless death must have been like to her family. Juneau seemed like such a "safe" place. People got drunk on Saturday nights down at the Red Dog Saloon and other dockside bars. Prostitutes were routinely arrested on Franklin Street, but few people even locked their doors before the murder. A murder in Juneau in broad daylight was unconscionable. As I walked past Mother's office building on my way home from school that day, police were carrying Mrs. Cornell's body to a waiting hearse.

Juneau didn't need TV with its surplus of crime dramas; rather, this was our own local drama playing out before our very eyes.

The tragedy at Mother's office and the death of my good friend were wake up calls that life can change in a moment and from that time forward, never be the same again. Losing my friend was heartbreaking and sad, but knowing that Mother could have easily been the one shot was sobering. Our safe little town was violated that September day when one crazy man shattered the peacefulness of our little world in an instant.

Chapter 16
Missing Pieces

Life in Southeast Alaska was great. Glaciers, mountains, the sea, and deserted gold mines were plentiful. Wild flowers and exotic birds, eagles, and even bears were seen nearly every day. Even though we had little money, and despite the incessant rain, our family had incredible experiences in this unimaginably beautiful locale. I always felt a bit sorry for our visitors. They visited Juneau for a day or two, and during those days Mom and Dad did everything they could to squeeze in as much sightseeing as possible. A brief trip to the glacier was a must. Those trips, though, were very similar to today's organized tours. We'd drive to the glacier, get out of the car and walk around a while, and then return to town. There was never time for the in depth and impromptu hiking that our family could do whenever we wished. We were, indeed, fortunate to live in Juneau.

Despite all the beauty and accessibility to nature, sometimes I still felt deprived living in Juneau. My feelings were normal: If you live in the mountains, you want to be at the beach. If you live in the city, you want to live on the farm. If you are tall, you want to be short, etc. It's just human nature to wistfully look at greener grass on the other side of the fence. Two missing pieces that I was certain weren't part of my life in Juneau were television and summer camp. There was NO television in Juneau at all, but there was a lot of camping. Our family, though, didn't camp, and I didn't belong to scouts. Therefore, I thought I was really missing out on some huge pieces of a "normal" childhood in the states.

Dad was pretty strict, and he believed that anything extracurricular should be sponsored by the church. That's okay, if you have a church. But, we didn't have a church like the one in Ohio. Not at all; we had a struggling little mission. We picnicked a lot because it was free; just like skiing, though, we couldn't afford camping equipment.

The mission had no funds to provide organized activities such as summer camps and kids' after school programs. I was so busy in school, practicing the piano, and cooking dinner every night that I had little time for other activities anyway. One year I joined the 4-H Club and participated in their big fair down at the water front in a huge building we called the "Subport." It was from the Subport that each New Year's Eve the city fathers put off a gigantic pyrotechnic display. On the Fourth of July it was too light!

Mrs. Davis had already established the most successful concert series in the entire territory in our little town of Juneau. Dad and Mom sacrificed and purchased tickets for us to attend these concerts at the Twentieth Century Theater on Franklin Street. There, I witnessed some of the world's most outstanding musicians of the day. We dressed up as though we were in Manhattan attending an event at Carnegie Hall. After these concerts, Dad broke his "no eating out" rule and took us next door to the drug store for a sundae or a milkshake. These concerts were *huge* in my young life. In the summer of 1955, Mrs. Davis launched an aggressive summer music program for Juneau's citizens that promised to be a winner.

Mrs. Davis' summer music program was a brilliant idea. In 1955 Fred Waring and the "Singing Pennsylvanians" were a national rage. Through her many contacts, Mrs. Davis was able to negotiate with Fred Waring himself. Her ingenious idea rapidly won the attention of the entire area. She organized a children's choir, a junior high school choir, a high school choir, and an adult choir. I was in the junior high choir. Each choir had its own local leader, and each choir member paid a nominal fee for the Fred Waring music.

All summer we practiced weekly. This practicing would culminate in a giant concert at the Twentieth Century Theater at the end of summer. Each individual choir was scheduled to sing several songs, and the grand finale was the joint choir singing Fred Waring's own arrangement of Alaska's state song, "Eight Stars of Gold on a Field of Blue" (See Appendix No. 2). Fred Waring wasn't able to come, but he sent his right hand man—Earl Wilhoit—to direct Juneau's own homegrown concert. During the spring and summer of 1955, nearly everyone in Juneau focused on the upcoming Fred Waring Concert.

A year after Dad started the Juneau mission, one of his friends pioneered a similar mission in Ketchikan. This man had a daughter my age, and we became pen pals. In 1955 she wrote and invited me to come to Ketchikan to spend a week with her and attend summer camp. I was thrilled! Finally, I had an opportunity to experience summer camp. The only hitch, however, was money. The cost of the camp was minimal, but I had to fly to Ketchikan first, and that was expensive. Mom and Dad wanted me to go but didn't have money for a plane ticket.

During my sixth grade year, I began babysitting and soon had quite a little business. I had saved some money, but not nearly enough for a plane ticket. Could it be possible, I thought, that after dreaming of summer camp so long that I would come so close and then miss it just because of money? I decided not! In the summer of 1955, Mrs. Davis made an offer to any kid in town who wanted to make a little extra money. She would pay a few cents for each ticket they sold to the big August concert. This was my opportunity to attend camp, and I went after it in a big way.

For weeks, I went door to door selling tickets to the concert. I have no memory of how many tickets I ultimately sold, but my recollection is that I sold more than any other kid in town—a whole lot more! When I added the ticket sale money to the babysitting money, I had enough to pay for the plane ticket and the cost of the camp—by myself. Ironically, I almost missed camp because of the concert. If we missed practice, we couldn't be in the concert. It was that simple; Mrs. Davis was serious about what she did and was determined that the concert be top quality. In the end, I think she took pity on me and made an exception, because I had to miss a practice when I flew to Ketchikan and summer camp.

Flying to Ketchikan in 1955 was different than it is today. Jets now land on Gravina Island across the Tongass Narrows in clear view of Ketchikan. A small ferry shuttles people and cargo back and forth several times daily. In 1955 my Pan American plane ticket was from Juneau to Annette Island—not Ketchikan. Annette is several miles south of Ketchikan just inside the United States border (See Appendix No. 3). It was on this island that our Pan American plane crashed in Oct. 1947 (See *Little House in the Arctic,* Chapter 2). From Annette, I boarded a Grumman Goose and flew north to Ketchikan.

The Grumman Goose was one of Alaska's most unique flying machines. Left behind after World War II, these old warhorses were conscripted into all kinds of service in the years following the war. In the 1950s there were only two methods to get to Ketchikan: boat or Grumman Goose. The Goose can land and take off on either land or water, but it has no pontoons. What made it different from today's common pontoon planes is that when it landed on the water, it landed on its belly. When the Goose hit the water, it shot up a rooster tail like you have never seen.

On Annette Island I transferred from the big modern Pan Am plane to this war relic. There were six passengers; five nuns and me. The noise of the plane was deafening, and I decided to try an experiment. Between Annette and Ketchikan, I sang as loudly as I could, yet none of the nuns acted like she heard me. The Goose landed at Ketchikan's wharf beside famous Creek Street. The door flew open; I stepped out and jumped across the water to the dock where my friend and her parents were waiting. I was only twelve, but Mom and Dad trusted me and knew that even then I was independent enough to make such a trip by myself.

Ketchikan is on Revillagigedo Island and you arrive via the Tongass Narrows. Across the Clarence Strait is Prince of Wales Island—the third largest island in the United States. A few miles south of Ketchikan are the world famous and spectacular Misty Fjords. As far as you can see, there is one island after another. I saw totem poles when I visited Sitka in 1952; Juneau has them in front of the Governor's Mansion; but Ketchikan has more totem poles than anywhere else in Southeast Alaska; they are everywhere.

One direction from town is the famous Saxman Village and in the other direction is Totem Bite. We visited Saxman Village, and I was in awe as I stood before the brightly decorated tribal house with its distinctive Native American symbols. Not only does Ketchikan have totem poles galore, but it is the salmon capital of the world. Its broad banner declaring Ketchikan "The Salmon Capital of the World" spans a street downtown near the docks and has been a Ketchikan icon for well over sixty years.

Several local Ketchikan churches collaborated for this camp—including the Salvation Army. After church on Sunday, I boarded a cabin cruiser with my friend Edie and several other pre-teens. The day was unusually sunny. We traveled by water most of the day until we reached the island camp. And what a camp it was. It wasn't anything like the modern, upscale camps kids attend today. Rather, it consisted of several rustic unheated cabins and one large community building that was used for eating and meetings. The camp was situated between the edge of the forest and the shores of the island. We hiked in the woods, dug clams, studied the Bible, sang camp songs by a campfire, and washed our own dishes. It was a fairy tale experience—including the deer outside our cabins each morning.

When that magical week of camp came to an end, I jumped onto the Grumman Goose at the Ketchikan wharf and reversed my trip to Annette and back to Juneau. A few days after I returned to, Juneau, I participated in the big Fred Waring concert celebration. The concert was major for our little town, but something else even bigger and more revolutionary was headed our way that year.

TELEVISION. Yes, that's right; television and progress were headed to Juneau. When we visited the states for Christmas 1949, Jason and I saw TV for the first time. During our year in Ohio, some of our neighbors had TV. Occasionally, we got to view a show, but we certainly didn't own a TV. That was never even a point of discussion in our house. Now technology was coming to Juneau, but in a typically unique Alaskan style. Even though I knew that Dad couldn't afford to buy a TV, and probably wouldn't buy one if he could, I was excited. Maybe—just maybe—I would get to see a show once in a while.

Television was coming to Juneau—canned TV, that is. Even canned TV created a big local "to do." In retrospect it wasn't such a big deal. There were no stores in Juneau that sold TVs, so anyone who bought a set had to purchase it in Seattle or somewhere else on the West Coast. Canned TV was unique. Pre-selected "canned" programs and their airing times were posted in the *Daily Alaska Empire* (Now the *Juneau Empire*) and announced on the radio. You had no selection of shows. One night we were invited to the neighbor's house to view the "Ed Sullivan Show." Their house was full that night as we crowded around a small black and white TV and watched a show that had been aired in the states several weeks earlier. We didn't care; this was progress and Juneau was becoming less isolated.

One night while I was babysitting, I was thrilled when I arrived to discover that the people owned a TV. I could hardly wait to put the kids to bed because if you missed the time of a show, all you would see was static. I was rewarded that night, though, when I turned on the TV and watched an episode of a situation comedy called "Duffy's Tavern." If those people would have known how delighted I was about being able to watch TV, they could have gotten away without paying me a cent.

Camp and TV were two missing commodities from my life. Juneau, though, had one threat that we would be glad to put behind us forever. When we lived in Fairbanks during the Korean War, we grew accustomed to air raids and blackouts. Fairbanks was the first line of defense against the Red Menace, and it was imperative that we be prepared. By the time we arrived in Juneau, the Korean War was history, but that ground war was rapidly replaced by the Cold War. The Russians were still coming, and we were still the first line of defense. We had to be prepared for anything. The constant paranoia of having this hang over our heads was wearing.

One specific event underlined this exaggerated corporate paranoia. For days we were told to prepare for a practice evacuation. Juneau, the authorities said, could be bombed, and it was necessary that we have an evacuation plan. The newspaper and the radio station published and announced the escape route. The practice day was chosen, and everyone was forewarned. It was compulsory that every citizen in Juneau comply. They made believers of us all, and our family knew the drill.

Early one morning before the sun came up, a loud whistle blew continually until every single person in town was awakened. We had been previously instructed that when the whistle blew, we were to head for our cars and follow the published evacuation route. Anyone who did not have a car was to dress and stand on a corner until a neighbor picked him or her up. Homes would be checked; every single one must be vacant; that was the decree.

And so people complied. This practice evacuation turned out to be a boondoggle and a huge laughing matter. Egan Road is now a lovely four lane highway that leads from downtown toward the airport in the valley. In 1955, there was only a winding two lane road in that direction. Every single car, truck, and moving vehicle in Juneau was headed on the same road in the same direction. It was a major traffic jam, but that wasn't the laughable part. Our destination was the airport runway. Civil defense "experts" were at the airport directing traffic and lining cars up side by side on the tarmac—the largest flat area in the entire region. Even as a twelve year old I could see the absurdity of it all. If the enemy had chosen to bomb Juneau that morning, they could have decimated every single resident with one shot. Needless to say, such an exercise in futility was never repeated.

Like any pre-teen any place, I was convinced that living in Juneau was depriving me of several important childhood experiences. I filled in one perceived missing piece in my life when I attended summer camp in Ketchikan; that helped! The absence of TV was another missing piece, and the final arrival of TV in Juneau made me feel like a normal American kid. It didn't seem to matter that we didn't own a TV, or that there was really no choice of programs to watch. Alaska was modernizing, and I was a part of all the excitement. One piece of excitement, however, that I was anxious to leave behind was all the hoopla over Civil Defense. After eight years of living with the Russian cloud hanging ominously over my head, I was anxious to put that behind me and lead a normal life.

Chapter 17
Back to the States

Dad's 1953 return to Alaska was sincere. All of us loved our Fairbanks experience and naively expected Juneau to be more of the same. Looking back from the perspective of time, none of us would trade our years in Juneau, but it really wasn't the happy, carefree life we had all loved so dearly in Fairbanks. Life in Juneau was difficult in many respects and for several different reasons.

In the first place, Dad was a highly motivated, hard working, results oriented individual. None of his hard work and high motivation seemed to pay off while we were in Juneau. Later, he said that he felt that during his three years in Juneau he had been "plowing in the sand." In truth, Dad's hard worked did pay off. Now, over fifty years after those difficult early days, the Juneau church that he "dug out" is thriving. They have beautiful property in the valley near Mendenhall Glacier that houses a good sized sanctuary, a beautiful parsonage, and a small private park. More importantly, there is a strong congregation who attend the church.

There was no church when we arrived in Juneau, and little was there when we left. Dad purchased the first parsonage, chartered the mission, and established a small congregation. Any person's life work is only fully realized when look-ing back with the advantage of time; with that perspective, Dad's time in Juneau was not wasted. All that being said, Dad's efforts in starting the

The Juneau Mission Charter Sunday – 1954

mission in Juneau were difficult for him. For his own sanity and sense of self-respect, he needed to get back to an aggressive and forward moving congregation.

Life in Juneau from the day we arrived until the day we left was difficult for all of us. Living in the boarding house that first year stretched us to our extremities; perhaps it set the stage for life in general in Juneau. Jason and Sammy had an age difference of seven years and a huge difference in personalities; I seemed to be caught in between. As Jason approached his teenage years, Mother and Dad began to feel that it was only fair to both him and me to return to the states. They wanted to provide us with opportunities and activities that they felt were missing in our little mission.

Mother was good at her job, and yet that, too, was a strain on home and family life. She always worked side by side with Dad in all of his churches, and that fact didn't change even though she worked a forty hour week. I think if I hadn't learned to cook during my fifth grade year in the boarding house, our family might not have made it at all. Jason, too, did a great deal of the housekeeping, and that was an immense help. Mother was an excellent employee; worked her fingers to the bone at home; and worked with Dad just like she had always done. Many nights after dinner, they got in the little Chevy and went "calling." *Calling* was the term they used when they visited people from the mission and encouraged them to return.

After Glen and Shirley arrived in Juneau from Illinois, they became Mom and Dad's constant companions. They were family. They worked tirelessly in the mission, and the two of them and their children brought us all companionship and joy. Late in 1955, Glen and Shirley decided that their job in the Juneau mission was completed and that they needed to return to Illinois to be near their families. That was the right thing for them to do; but it was a blow to our family. When they left, there was a huge hole both in the mission and in our family. We missed them dearly, and I think they're leaving jump started Dad's final decision to leave Alaska.

By early 1956, then, Dad determined that we would leave Alaska when school was out that spring. He contacted his denominational supervisor like he had done in 1952 and waited for a new assignment. Dad's supervisor in 1956 was a different man than his supervisor in 1952. He was a wonderful man and had visited our home and our mission, and yet he never fully understood how difficult it was. He must have thought that Dad couldn't handle anything of significance because the mission was so small. Consequently, all he offered Dad in the states were tiny little churches. Dad wasn't "too good" for that, but I think he felt that he could handle more, and so he held out for a better offer. Unfortunately, a "better offer" never arrived, but his plans to leave Alaska progressed just the same.

Dad and Mom knew that the little 1952 Chevy had fulfilled its usefulness as far as we were concerned. It had certainly stood us in good stead. It carried us safely across the United States twice; both in 1952 and again in 1953. It was our only form of transportation for three solid years in Juneau, and after those three years, it wasn't worth shipping back to the states. One more time Mom and Dad contacted Seattle car dealerships for new car brochures. Again, our home was filled with new car shopping excitement.

After weeks of pouring over shiny brochures, Dad and Mom chose a 1956 Chevrolet 210 four door sedan for our next automobile. We had had our fill of two door cars; there would never be another! We couldn't afford the upscale Chevrolet Bel Air that was so popular in 1956, but the Chevy 210 was pretty snazzy compared to the little coupe. Dad and Mom selected the popular two-toned combination that was the brand new style and all the rage. Our new car would be white and turquoise, but we had to wait a long time before we got to see it.

During our final year in Juneau—my seventh grade year—we older grade school girls were allowed to cross the school yard bridge and walk a block down Sixth Street to the high school. There we attended home economics classes, and it was there that I became part of the band. One six weeks a group of us girls decided that we didn't like the Home Ec. teacher, and we purposely gave her fits. We teased her, deliberately asked stupid questions, and overall were not nice. All of us were good students; and I think we thought there was safety in numbers. We were wrong. When report cards came out, ALL of us were shocked. The Home Ec. teacher had the final say about our poor deportment when she gave each and every one of us a "D" in conduct.

All the other girls thought it was funny and were laughing about it on the way home—that is all the girls except me and one other. I knew that Mom and Dad wouldn't think a "D" was funny—not one bit. I was braced for the gavel to fall when I showed them my report card, yet I really had no idea what my punishment would be. Both Jason and I generally got straight "A's." No one ever got a "C," and a "D" was unheard of. I knew I was a goner that day as I trudged past the governor's mansion, down the hill, and home to Mom and Dad.

Mom and Dad were so disappointed in me that I felt even worse. Parents didn't use the term "grounded" in 1956, but for all intents and purposes, that's what happened to me. Until new report cards came out six weeks later, I couldn't go to any of my friends' homes. I had to stay home, practice the piano, help around the house, and behave myself. It may sound odd, but the biggest restriction I had during those six weeks was that I couldn't go to the library. Jason and I loved going to the library, so this was huge to me. You better believe that when report cards came out again, my conduct grade was UP. The teacher couldn't bring herself to give me an "A" because I was so bad the six weeks before, but Mom and Dad were satisfied with the "B" I received. It signified to them that I had corrected the errors of my ways.

My experience at the high school in the band was much more positive than my Home Ec. experience. Since the third grade I had taken piano lessons, but I really wanted to learn another instrument. Mother and Dad were clear that they couldn't afford to buy or rent an instrument, and they didn't think I had the time to practice a second instrument anyway. Nevertheless, when a new band director came to town, I went over to the high school and asked him if he had any instruments available that I could learn. He offered to let me borrow the school's oboe for that year, and Mom and Dad rather unenthusiastically agreed. When I couldn't read the music well enough to play the oboe, the director let me play the base drum and sometimes the snare.

Truthfully, I wasn't good at any of the three. That's a fact; I knew it then, and I know it today. But, the band director liked me a lot and asked me to be the student conductor of the band. I still don't know what it was about me that caused him to like me so. Many of the other kids had been in band for three years, and the position of student conductor was a pretty big deal. Nevertheless, I got the job. It was great fun to take the baton and lead the band in at least one number at every concert. Mom and Dad were surprised by my new found talent of leading the band, and they were proud. That was the only experience in my entire life at conducting, but it was still fun. In fact, it was a "hoot."

What I enjoyed the most, though, was singing. The year I was in seventh grade, the grade school hired a new music teacher. I loved her as much as I liked the band director. The music teacher organized a triple trio, and I was selected as a member. We got to sing at school events, around town, and once I even sang a solo on the radio. But, the biggest perk of being in the triple trio was the fact that we practiced at noon. All my life until then, I attended schools where we had to go home for lunch, and in Alaska it's a lot of work to walk back and forth twice a day. Each time I went outside, I had to bundle up in layers of clothing, fight the wind, and then reverse the process on the other end. When the triple trio practiced, though, we were allowed to bring a sack lunch. It sounds silly, but I thought it was a big deal to eat at school!

Both at Christmas and again in the spring, the band, choir, and triple trio presented concerts for our parents. Mother and Dad considered these concerts as important as Mrs. Davis' big concerts with world famous musicians. For each concert, Jason and I got new clothes, and when the concert was over, Dad took us downtown to the drugstore for a treat. Music and musical events were always primary to Mom and Dad, and Jason and I loved being a part of them.

Basketball was Alaska's biggest team sport in the fifties, and it still is today. In order to compete, teams travel many miles across the state by air and ferry. During my seventh grade year I developed a lifelong love of basketball. Whenever there was a home game on Friday night, Dad let me walk up the hill to the high school with my friends. I really got into it. When a visiting team from Anchorage or Fairbanks or one of Southeast Alaska's island cities came to town, just about everyone in Juneau showed up at the high school gym for the big game. The gym's smallness never dampened the spirit of Juneau's citizens. It would be unthinkable now to let a group of twelve year old girls walk alone in the dark to and from a ball game, but in Juneau in 1956, few people thought much of it at all—even after the murder at Mother's office.

By the spring of 1956, my seventh grade year was rapidly coming to an end. I was excited to return to the states even though it was an anxious time since none of us knew where we were moving. In April before we left, Mom and Dad bought plane tickets for all five of us to fly to Fairbanks for the big territorial church convention. Jason and I didn't care much about the convention, yet this was our first trip back to Fairbanks since our departure in 1952. We were eager both to see our Fairbanks friends and other friends from different missions around the territory. Our refueling spot was White Horse just like it was in 1947 when we were diverted from Annette Island because of the big storm (See *Little House in the Arctic* Chap. 2).

Our preparations for leaving Juneau were simple. Mom and Dad were leaving pretty much like we came, except this time we weren't even taking a car. We arrived in Juneau with a few clothes and personal items, and that's how we left. Everything else was left behind—our furniture, my doll collection, and even our little cocker spaniel, Blondie. Dad purchased plane tickets to Seattle so we could take delivery of another new car, and there wasn't extra money for cargo. Besides that, Dad still didn't have a job when we left town—there was no where to send things if we had wanted to.

Taking delivery of a new car in Seattle was becoming rather routine for our family. In 1949 we picked up the Ford Woody; in 1952 we picked up the little Chevy coupe; and now in

1956 Chevrolet 210

1956 we were getting a beautiful new Chevrolet 210 four door sedan. Because Mom and Dad were attending another big convention in Kansas City in early June, we had to leave Juneau a couple days before school was dismissed. The last morning that we had breakfast in the house at the bottom of Ninth Street Hill, we ate on old mismatched dishes. When we finished, we didn't wash the dishes; we simply threw them away. I loved that!

Our plane for Seattle was scheduled for a mid-afternoon departure. Before we left Juneau, Dad treated us to a rare treat that surprised everyone; we went downtown Juneau to the Baranof Hotel for lunch. Other than our after concert treats at the drug store, that was the only time we ate out during our entire three years in Juneau. It was indeed a treat to sit in the elegant dining room of Juneau's finest hotel and dine like the rich folks. Shortly, it was time to leave for the airport and our departure from Alaska.

Once more we boarded a Pan Am plane and set our sights southward. In a few hours we landed in the metropolis of Seattle—an entirely different world from Juneau. That day presented yet another surprise. When Dad went to the dealership to take delivery of the new Chevrolet, it wasn't ready and wouldn't be available for another day. The mistake was theirs, not ours, so they provided us a room in a luxurious Seattle hotel. Anything would have seemed big to me after Juneau, but across the street from the hotel was a truly big department store. That day was the first day I ever saw an escalator. It was wooden and would be considered a relic today, but in 1956, this new moving stairway was cutting edge technology. Wow! Earlier in the day I ate at one of Alaska's finest hotels, and now I was lodging in style in a beautiful hotel in the big city of Seattle. How quickly things changed!

We left Seattle mid-day the next day—May 22, 1956, just a few days shy of my thirteenth birthday. One last time Dad got behind the wheel of a brand new car in Seattle, and we set our direction south toward Longview, Medford, and points beyond. We were in a hurry, because this year Dad and Mom planned to take us with them to the big church convention in Kansas City, and I could hardly wait.

It would be two long months before Dad had a place to settle. Just in time for school and the beginning of eighth grade, we moved back to Oklahoma where Mom and Dad and I were all born. Our return "home" to Oklahoma, though, only last two and a half years. The West Coast was in our blood by then, and in January of 1959, Dad moved the family back west. This time we moved to Spokane, Washington. Spokane wasn't Alaska, but it sure was closer than Oklahoma!

Just like that, our Alaska odyssey was history. And yet, the odyssey continues. Once you visit Alaska, a part of you never goes all the way back home. It was several decades after 1956 that I returned to Alaska physically for the first time; nevertheless, I returned hundreds of times in my memory. Alaska has a way of taking hold of you and never letting go. In my adult years, I now have the unspeakable privilege of visiting Alaska all summer, every summer, and sharing stories and a bit of knowledge about this amazing land with hundreds of people from every country in the world. Who would have thought those many years ago that such a thing would ever happen? Not me.

Whether you've been to Alaska only once; whether you've never been; whether you spent time there in the service or as a child; or whether you spent a life time in Alaska, you will never fully know her. Alaska is bigger than the combination of all of us. Although Alaska is our largest state, it isn't crowded. There is one square mile of Alaska for each and every person living there. She is so huge that one description will never define her and her many different ecosystems. She is bigger than life. Alaska is most assuredly a land of contrasts.

John Muir describes Alaska better than anyone: *For the lover of pure wildness, Alaska is one of the most wonderful countries in the world. No other experience can be made to any other country in the world where an abundance of noble scenery is so charmingly brought to men. No words can convey anything like an adequate conception of Alaska's sublime grandeur... it is only the natural effect of appreciable manifestations of the presence of God.* Wherever you go in Alaska—the temperate rainforests, the Aleutian Islands, the frigid interior, the big city of Anchorage, the Bering Sea, or the arid tundra, you will discover something spiritual. Alaska silently brings us up short and reminds us that we are never ever just human beings having a spiritual experience. Visiting and experiencing and breathing Alaska reminds us that we are first and always spiritual beings, and that this life is only a mere fleeting human experience. I love Alaska!

Appendix

NUMBER 1
Alaska's State Flag

When Alaska was purchased in 1867 from Russia, it had no symbols whatsoever. Even after it received territorial status, Alaska had no flag. In 1927 the governor decided this must be rectified. The American Legion sponsored a flag designing contest for 7th graders through high school students. Hundreds of entries were submitted for review. The winning design was an instant hit with Alaskans and remains so to this day.

Alaska's flag is the quintessential example of "less is more." It was submitted by Benny Benson, a thirteen year old boy from Unalaska far down the Aleutians. The son of an Aleut mother and a Norwegian father, Benny was in the Presbyterian mission school in Seward when he submitted his design on a piece of cardboard. His simple design of "eight stars of gold on a field of blue" was inspired by his many nights sitting by the ocean in Unalaska and studying the stars. The blue represents the sea and sky; the gold represents Alaska's wealth.

Benny was an Alaskan folk hero from then until his death in 1972. He was awarded a gold watch with the flag design inside the watch case and a trip to Washington DC to meet President Coolidge; however, the trip never took place. He is buried in California.

NUMBER 2

Alaska's State Song

Eight stars of gold on a field of blue -

Alaska's flag may it mean to you.

The blue of the sea; the evening sky.

The mountain lakes and the flow'rs near by.

The gold of the early sourdough's dreams,

The precious gold of the hills and streams;

The brilliant stars in the northern sky:

The "Bear" - the "Dipper" - and shining high.

The great North Star with its steady light

O'er land and sea, a beacon bright.

Alaska's flag - to Alaskans dear

The simple flag of a last frontier.

In 1935 Marie Drake's poem about Benny Benson's winning flag design was featured on the cover of a Territorial Education Publication. Ellen Dusenbury, wife of the Chilkoot barracks commander in Haines, later put the poem to music. In 1955 it was declared Alaska's official state song. The upright piano that it was composed on is displayed in Skagway's historic Pullam House. Park Rangers still allow tourists to play the piano.

Alaskan's are proud of their state song with its beautiful words and singable melody. It is frequently sung throughout the state by schools, children, and adult choirs. Anyone living in Alaska for any length of time is familiar with this lovely state song.

NUMBER 3

Annette Island and Metlakatla

In 1887 an Anglican missionary named William Duncan had a disagreement with the powers that be on Metlakatla in Canada. Subsequently, he moved his mission and many of his followers across the U.S. border to Annette Island. He named the settlement the "New Metlakatla." This island that is situated twenty air miles south of Ketchikan lies just inside the United States boundary near Prince Rupert, British Columbia. It was a strategic location during World War II.

When Pearl Harbor was attacked, the U. S. and Canada had just begun a joint defense plan. The port of Prince Rupert was strategic for Canada, but it was difficult to defend. In the late 1930s Civilian Conservation Corps workers constructed an airfield on Annette. During 1941 and 1942, the Army Corps of Engineers expanded the project, and Annette became a necessary refueling location for military flights. When Pan Am began to fly "Clippers" to Alaska after the war, Annette was again used as a refueling spot for commercial flights.

It was on Annette's Mt. Tamgas that the Pan Am plane my family had been on two days earlier crashed Oct. 26, 1947 (See *Little House in the Arctic,* Chap. 2). Annette Island was used extensively through the 1960s as a landing spot for Grumman Gooses and Alaskan commercial flights. After the airport opened on Gravina Island across from Ketchikan, Annette became more quiet. William Healey Dall, the famed naturalist, named the island after his wife, Annette.

NUMBER 4

The Grumman Goose

The Grumman Goose was designed in 1937 in Bethpage, New York as an amphibious transport for Manhattan millionaires to get back and forth to their yachts. It was soon recognized as a method of transportation with many uses. The first civilian models carried two to three passengers and had a small onboard bar and toilet. As the plane evolved, it was able to carry more passengers and cargo.

Because it was amphibious, had ample interior space, and rugged construction, the Goose could fly nearly anywhere. In 1938, the U. S. Coast Guard first used the Goose as a rescue plane, and it soon became a military workhorse. During the Forgotten War in the Aleutians, the Goose (Army OA-9) was suited for multiple uses. After World War II several hundred Gooses were abandoned in Alaska. Enterprising Alaskans purchased them, and they were used extensively in the territory until the early 1960s. It was a Grumman G-21A that I flew back and forth from Annette Island to Ketchikan. It was also a Goose that crashed on Admiralty Island with Mrs. Davis' daughter aboard.

NUMBER 5

Seymour Narrows

A little over one hundred miles north of Vancouver is *the* most treacherous section of the Inside Passage—the Seymour Narrows. Until 1958, this section of waters claimed hundreds of lives and dozens of ships. Protruding nearly to the water's surface was a sharp mountain peak called "Ripple Rock." At low tide, the tip of the peak was only nine feet below the surface. Captains—even today—must calculate the tide through this area and schedule their sailing times accordingly. Many attempts were made to destroy "Old Rip," but it wasn't until 1958 (five years after our voyage) that it was at last wiped off the map for ever.

The method of destroying the rock was ingenious. In a sense, engineers performed a geological "root canal." On Maud Island across from the city of Campbell River, they drilled a 400 foot shaft straight down; they then drilled a 2,400 foot tunnel across the ocean floor, followed by another 325 foot shaft that went directly into the core of the rock. They packed the shafts with 1,375 tons of explosives, and at 9:31 AM, April 5, 1958, they blew thirty-six feet of the rock to kingdom come. The blast pulverized 370,000 tons of rock and displaced 320,000 tons of water. It was the largest non-nuclear blast in the history of the world. After years of speculating about the dangers of such a blast, it was rather uneventful. A few bug-eyed fish were the only casualties. Within a few hours, everything was calm and ships were sailing easily through the narrows.

Acknowledgements

The Alaska State Library

The Daily Alaska Empire (Juneau Empire)

Travis Davis Photography

Dedman's Photography (Skagway)

The Juneau-Douglas City Museum

The Juneau Public Library

John Muir: *Travels in Alaska*

National Bicycle History Archive of America

The Perseverance & Alaska Gastineau
Gold Mining Company Video

Letitia Thomas Photography

Kathy Slamp's other Alaska Books:

Go to www.alaskathy.com
or call (316) 204-1234

Little House in the Arctic   *A Picnic at the Glacier*
$17.95 $10.95

Rendezvous with Majesty: *Majesty Alaska DVD*
Alaska's Amazing Glaciers! $19.95
$9.95

Check out Kathy's other website for a list of other books.

Go to www.vesselministries.com

Mailing address available on websites.

ORDER FORM:
Please mail my copy/copies to:

Name _____

Street _____

City _____

State _____ Zip _____

	QTY.	PRICE
Little House in the Arctic – $17.95 per book		
Little House in the Rain Forest – $17.95 per book		
Rendezvous with Majesty: Alaska's Amazing Glaciers – $9.95 per book		
A Picnic at the Glacier – $10.95 per book		
Majesty Alaska DVD – $19.95		
Shipping/handling: $3.00 per book		
	TOTAL	

You may pay with Visa, MC, or check.

Card No. _____ Exp. Date _____

Signature _____